F(

1815 Adams Rd. Summit Lake, British Columbia

ISBN: 978-1-9990562-0-9

Printed and Bound in Canada by Blitzprint Inc.

Map of Project Area kindly developed by Jean-Yves Landry.
www.humanecology.ca

All photos and poems by author, Hilary Crowley

Map of South India on page 6 taken from internet site, with permission.

Hilary Crowley

Dedicated to Samuha Samarthya
and all the families living with disability
in India and elsewhere.

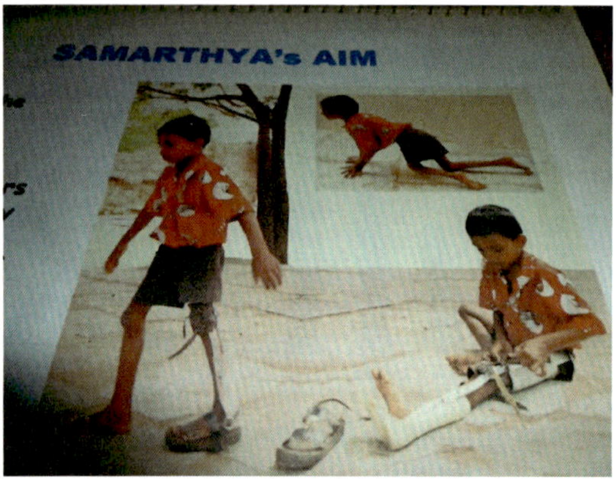

Virupakshi – from crawl to walk

All profits from this book will support Samuha Samarthya's Disability Program

REVIEW

FOOTSTEPS TO FREEDOM:

I loved reading this book and was hooked from the first page. Beautifully written! A rich blend of the exotic, the new & the unexpected interwoven with the northern rural routines of home. Portrayed experiences are interesting, very engaging and flow well. Poetic, honest and straight from the heart. Richly described scenes are so evocative and resonant that they make the reader feel that they are right there, sharing the experience, and feeling the transformations over time. Comparisons and contrasts are strikingly vivid, well balanced, refreshingly non-judgemental, and seasoned from time to time with a touch of humor. I loved the chapter titles with quotations that hinted to the coming content. An intensely personal journey of travel, bravery, generosity, ingenuity, professional dedication and transformation; the inspiring story of one physio to "Never miss an opportunity" to make the world a better place.

Judy Lett BScN, MSc, RN (retired).

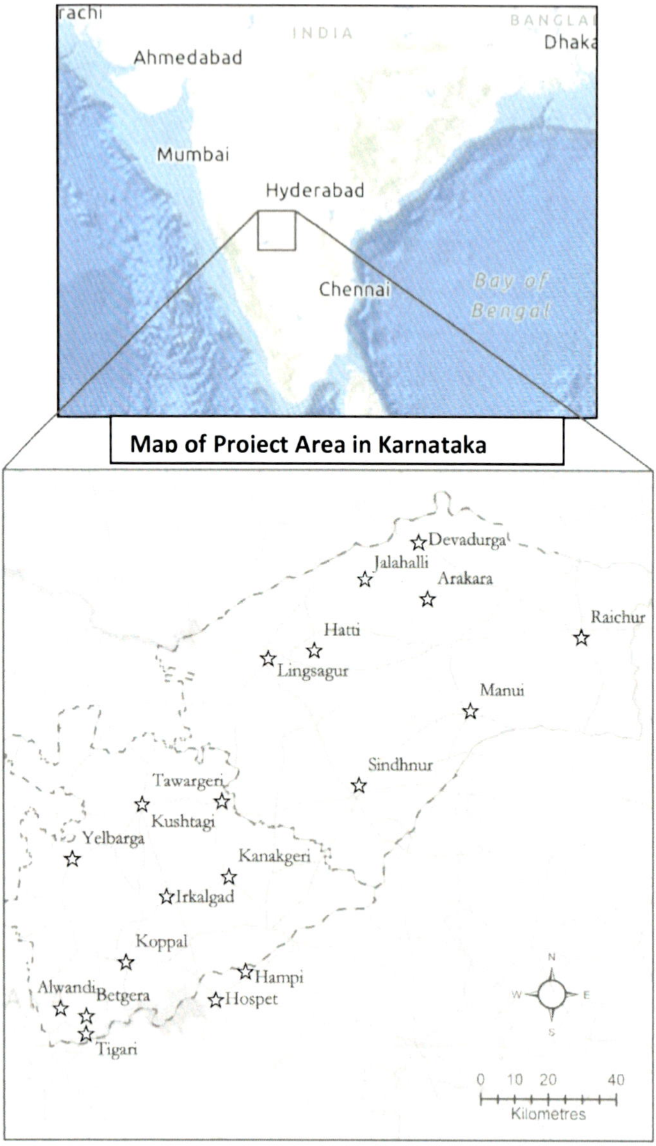
rachi
INDIA
BANGLA
Dhaka
Ahmedabad
Mumbai
Hyderabad
Chennai
Bay of Bengal
Map of Project Area in Karnataka
Devadurga
Jalahalli
Arakara
Raichur
Hatti
Lingsagur
Manui
Sindhnur
Tawargeri
Kushtagi
Yelbarga
Kanakgeri
Irkalgad
Koppal
Hampi
Hospet
Alwandi
Betgera
Tigari
N
W
E
S
0 10 20 40
Kilometres

CONTENTS

Part 1: Year in India April 1994- June 1995

Part 2: Annual Trips to India with Evolution of Samuha and S.O.D.A.

Part 3: Twenty Four Years Later

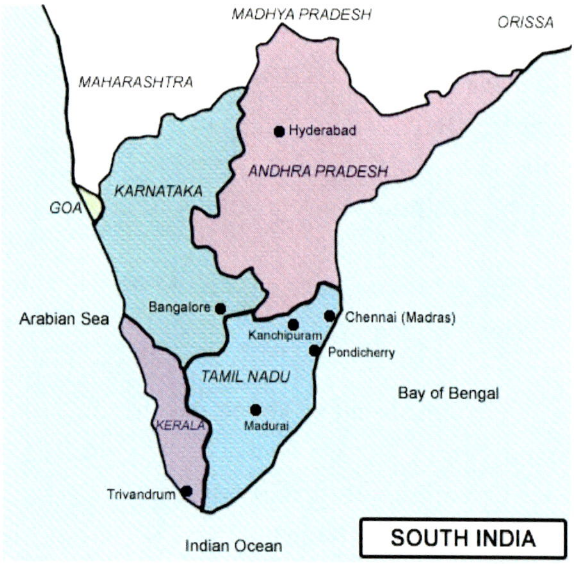

ACKNOWLEDGEMENTS:

I have many people to thank who helped bring this story to fruition. My sister, Helen, for her unflagging enthusiasm and encouragement. My husband, Floyd, for giving me the freedom to pursue my dreams. Narayanswamy and all the staff at Samuha Samarthya who inspired me with their dedication to their work and for being my second family. All the families with disability in India, who welcomed me into their homes. All the members of SODA and our supporters who enable this work to continue. Sheila, who gave me time off work to go to India.

Thank you to all those who helped me with writing advice; Helen, Floyd, Narayanswamy, Phil Sheppard, Lynne Peppler, Paul Swennumson, Joyce Helweg, Mike Nash, Betsy Warland. Special thanks to Cathy Stonehouse and Island Mountain Arts who facilitated the writing course that got me started. Thanks to Rural Writers in Residence for their encouragement. Thank you to Jean-Yves for making a great map of the project area.

I should like to take this opportunity to thank my parents for giving me a wonderful start in life and for encouraging me to seize every opportunity that came my way. Also thank you to the physiotherapy profession, both in England and Canada, who have given me the skills needed to make a difference to the lives of families living with disability in India.

Lastly, thank you to my family in Canada for allowing my absences and for giving me a strong foundation to come back to when I return home. I love you all.

Hilary Crowley, Summit Lake, 2019

FOOTSTEPS TO FREEDOM

Tales of Therapy in Rural India

PART 1

YEAR IN INDIA: April 1994 – June 1995

1
HOME FROM AWAY

"Find Purpose. The means will follow."
Mahatma Gandhi

The road to my home in Summit Lake seemed so grey and lifeless after the vibrant colours of rural India. Where were all the bare-foot villagers walking down the road with both their agricultural tools and their food on their heads? There were no goats or sheep being herded down the road and no cattle or chickens to avoid. When I stopped at my Canadian grocery store, everyone seemed so huge.

In India I fitted in well with my height of 5ft 2in and modest build. The rural Indians were much thinner and of course darker skinned with dark brown hair but here in northern British Columbia, the locals were much taller and so much wider. I felt like a dwarf amongst giants. No-one walked anywhere and the only animals to be seen were dogs, except in farmer's fields. I missed the vibrancy and chatter, even the honking of horns.

My husband Floyd picked me up at the Prince George airport, together with our daughter, Brenda and her sons Dylan & Dusty, who gave me a huge hug. It was wonderful to feel so welcomed back into the fold after my long absence. Floyd and I chatted in the car on the fifty kilometre drive home, gathering glimpses of our separate activities but always competing with the talk-radio, I'd forgotten about that aggravation. Once we reached the northern outskirts of town, we travelled between farmers' fields where the Rockies loomed in the distance. The road then crossed the Salmon River before climbing over rolling hills and between dense forest towards Summit Lake. Traffic consisted mostly of loaded logging trucks with a steady stream of private cars waiting for their opportunity to pass in their hurry to get home, or wherever they were going.

Eventually we turned off the busy highway on to what used to be the old highway as it meandered its way across the tracks then over the pipeline before we eventually saw a glimpse of the lake. The road followed above the lake before turning down into our small community, past several houses and the community hall then our log house, situated amongst the trees, at the end of the road. Floyd had persuaded Brenda to clean the house for us before I came home so I didn't have to immediately start washing dishes and vacuuming, which was a great relief.

The first thing I did was to have a hot shower. What bliss after months of managing with a jug and bucket of lukewarm water. Even better was the flush toilet and roll of toilet paper. The absence of these was one of the most difficult things I experienced in India. The next thing I did was unpack my luggage and put most of the clothes in the laundry basket as washing them in a bucket of water with a bar of soap was not so effective.

Jalahalli village, where I had spent my year in India, was so dusty. We washed ourselves and our clothes daily but it would still be good to put them through the washing machine before storing my Indian clothes until my next trip. I just hoped I hadn't brought any of the crawly critters back with me in my pack. I shook it out outside and put it in the sun to air out. I had lived out of this pack for a year as there was nowhere to hang or store clothes in my hut.

I settled into my home life in rural BC in our log home, which Floyd and I had built ourselves, on the shore of Summit Lake. I planted the vegetable garden, almost as soon as I returned, so it would have enough time to produce before frosts started coming again. We still had meat in the freezer from Floyd's last moose hunting trip.

Shortly after my return, it was July 1st, a big holiday in Canada. All the family came to Summit Lake and it was wonderful to be surrounded by them all again. We now had eleven grandchildren, from four children, so we enjoyed a week-end of paddle-boating, canoeing and water skiing as well as sports events at the community hall, all so different from India but a wonderful way to get re-submerged into the Canadian culture.

Floyd & I resumed our normal life together, although we had both become accustomed to living apart and being independent. We managed to come to an amicable agreement through sharing of chores, social outings, family gatherings and hosting of events. I returned to work at the Prince George Regional Hospital and outwardly I resumed my old life but often thought back to what I had left behind in rural India.

2
ARRIVAL IN INDIA

"Be the change you wish to see in the world"
Mahatma Gandhi

A year previously, I had arrived in Delhi in sweltering heat. It was 47degrees C. The heat hit me in the face as I walked out of the airport doors. In no time, rivers of sweat were running down my body. Men kept insisting that I take their taxi but there was meant to be a bus to the domestic airport. I didn't want to entrust myself to some insistent taxi driver. How did I know where I might land up? This place felt so alien.

Men bustled round carrying baskets of food on their head. Gaily clad women elegantly wandered selling garlands of jasmine and marigolds. Beggars stretched their arms out complaining of empty bellies. Children stood and stared. Dogs scavenged in the streets and cows meandered amongst the traffic. Rickshaws weaved precariously amongst the motor bikes, which carried families of five, only the driver wearing a helmet. I nervously waited in the heat for a bus to materialize but eventually gave myself up to a taxi driver, feeling the unknown journey couldn't be any worse than the insistent demands for my money from all these vociferous merchants & beggars. I had to pay for my ticket before the journey began, not a good omen.

Gradually I relaxed as my senses were filled with new sights and smells. Whole families lived on the edge of the road as men pissed in the gutter and cows licked the garbage. Men cycled carrying an umbrella for shade while skinny mules clip-clopped down the street pulling a rickety cart, laden with branches of bananas, with a young boy flailing the whip. Cows with bones protruding at the hips slowly plodded down the street while flat carts of brightly coloured ochre and red powder carried the merchant sitting cross-legged amongst his wares. Women cradled their babies with their hands out to passers-by, as old men with bandaged remains of hands appealed for money. A make-shift cradle suspended from scaffolding in a construction site hovered over the brightly saried mother who carried a flat tray of clay on her head.

I reached my destination safely and tipped the driver who was unaware of all my trepidation. He told me of a restaurant where I could wait for my next flight. Thankfully, I walked into the air-conditioned room and a smartly dressed waiter showed me to an easy chair and brought me a deliciously fresh cool lime soda. After this welcome interlude, I proceeded towards the departure area for the four hour flight to Bangalore.

I'd always wanted to work overseas ever since a magical experience and memorable year in South Africa twenty five years earlier. Shortly after graduating as a physiotherapist, a colleague, Penny, and I discovered during a game of tennis that we both had relatives in South Africa and a yearning to travel. That night, on her way home, Penny provisionally booked our return tickets to Johannesburg, valid for one year. A month later we were on our way. Penny's uncle was arch-deacon of

Zululand so we had a unique glimpse of South African life during Nelson Mandela's incarceration on Robben Island. We worked and travelled round the country until our tickets expired. Now I wanted to return to a hot climate and primitive life, not as a tourist but to live there and to really experience it. This was now 1994.

Floyd & I had a good life in Canada and had been together over twenty years. One precipitous day in 1994, Floyd and I had a major disagreement, which we could not resolve. I decided that instead of staying home moping, I should turn this episode into an opportunity. The children were grown up and starting to raise families of their own so I now had a challenge presented to me. I could realise my dream of travel and hopefully be able to use my physiotherapy training in a developing part of the world where these skills were most needed.

"International Health Exchange", a magazine offering overseas placements for health professionals, presented an opportunity through Action Health for a physiotherapy trainer in rural South India for a six month assignment with Samuha. I chose this, rather than to Africa which I had always dreamt of, since their assignments were for two years which I felt would be more frightening and disruptive to my life. My application to volunteer with Samuha, a rural integrated development organization, was successful but then I was scared. I was already middle-aged.

I pondered, "Would I have a home to come back to after this six month assignment?"

"Would Floyd and I settle our differences?"
"Would I like India?"

I decided to take a six month leave of absence from my work as a physiotherapist in the Prince George Regional Hospital. I said "good-bye" to all my family and friends and left for England as that was where Action Health's head office was. I also needed to spend some time with my sister on their farm in Hertfordshire. There were three weeks between interview and departure date. Three weeks filled with doubts, questions, worries.

"Did I know enough about my field of physiotherapy to be helpful?"
"Would I get sick?" I didn't have time to have all the required immunizations.
"Would I get mugged, robbed?"
"Would I be lonesome?"
"What about the language." So many doubts, I so nearly changed my mind.

I took a week-end course in Cambridge on learning how to teach. This involved meeting with previous Action Health volunteers and being put in conflict situations and asked to problem solve the situation. I even took a lesson on a motor-bike as that was meant to be my means of transportation. I wiped out on that first trial and wound up travelling to India with bandaged wounds on my arm and leg. Thankfully I swallowed all my fears and finally I left.

In Bangalore I was met by Sandra, an English nurse, who was also a volunteer with Samuha, the organization where I would be working. Sandra was about fifty and had been with Samuha for a couple of months already. She later told me how she had recently lost her husband and struggled with adapting to the Indian culture. She struck me as being very British, which probably explained how we took a taxi to the Victoria Hotel, the most English hotel in town. We were ushered into our rooms, where a large cockroach crawled on the floor. There was a western toilet but no paper, not even a toilet roll holder. The bathroom was tiled with a puny shower, which dribbled cold water, and a bucket. I washed the best I could and gave myself up to sleep on the hard bed with the sheet wrapped around my shoulders so that the cockroaches couldn't find me.

I'd made it so far but what a foreign country, more foreign even than Africa. The first morning in India immediately aroused all the senses. First of all the loud call to morning prayers heard through the window at 5.30am. On stepping outside, there was the heat closely followed by the cacophony of chaotic traffic. At the hotel we had an English breakfast of pale toast and tea.

Sandra said, "We need to get you some Indian clothes, and then we are invited out for lunch at Rita's. She works for Samuha but her family live here in Bangalore and they want us to go there for lunch. After that we'll take the night train to Raichur then on to the project at Jalahalli."

We went off in search of some traditional Indian clothing as western dress is not acceptable in the villages and so I was introduced to Bangalore traffic. The most prolific vehicles were the motor bikes closely followed by the black and yellow three wheeler auto rickshaws which dart in and out of traffic in an alarming manner. Many locals wore scarves over their faces to avoid inhaling the fumes of these 2-stroke engines. Some ponies pulled carts loaded with lengths of pipe that stretched way in front of the horses head and way behind the back of the cart. Crossing the street, as a pedestrian, was a feat in itself. It occurred to me that a blind person would find it impossible to navigate these sidewalks as there are many big holes in the pavement ready to trip you.

We bought two salwar kamiz, baggy cotton pants with matching shapeless cotton dress. They would have to do. Because the project has no library, I was pleased to find some excellent book stores. I found “God of Small Things” by Arundhati Roy. I already had with me “Disabled Village Children” by David Werner, which was to be my Bible for teaching purposes during my stay.

I had been warned that Jalahalli had no international phone connections so next I went in search of an international pay phone so I could phone Floyd & my sister, Helen. Fortunately I found them both home so we could chat and I told them I had arrived safely and I didn’t know when the next opportunity for communication may arise.

We then took a rickshaw to Rita's through a myriad of winding streets, past market stalls, beggars and bicycles with auto-rickshaws darting about without any perceived pattern. Families of five travelled by motor-bike with mother in a sari sitting side-saddle holding an infant on her lap, another child sandwiched between her and her husband with the son sitting in front of Dad, helping him drive. No helmets between them and a zillion more bikes and rickshaws careened precariously around them. As we neared our destination, the streets got dirtier and animals wandered aimlessly letting vehicles avoid them rather than the other way around.

The driver told us that we had arrived so we stumbled out and walked down a dingy lane. Rita, a plump Indian lady, came out of her house and ushered us in. We bent down to get in the doorway and saw five children sitting on the floor watching TV. A bed lay in the corner and a single wooden table with three plain wooden chairs stood by the doorway. "Come in and sit down" said Rita.
"This is my Mother and we've cooked you some special chicken."

Both Rita and her mother wore brightly coloured saris. Rita's mother wore her grey hair tied back in a bun and smiled at us but we weren't able to converse as she didn't speak English and we hadn't learnt any Kannada, the local language.

We were offered a steaming pot of chicken and lentils. The children stared at us but said nothing. Rita and her mother insisted that we eat but they wouldn't eat with us.

The food was piping hot and we were given a tin plate but no utensils. What to do? I looked enquiringly at Sandra but she was no help. She didn't seem to know what to do either. After a few minutes of embarrassing stalling, I finally picked up a piece of chicken with my fingers and started eating. I just about choked. I love Indian food but I found this the spiciest food imagineable. Rita just smiled and offered us some water which her mother ladled out of an earthenware pitcher but this was my biggest worry – the water. Luckily I had enough foresight to bring some bottled water with me. We took an hour to consume this food, full of gristle and grease and hot spice, so hot. I was never so thankful as when it came time to leave and we could say our thank-yous and bid them farewell. "Thank you for coming," said Rita "I'll see you in Jalahalli next week."

We hailed a taxi to the station for the overnight train to Raichur, a dirty fortress town in Northern Karnataka on the Deccan Plateau, - about a two hour jeep ride from our final destination. The taxi drew up to Bangalore station and we were immediately surrounded by red-turbaned porters wanting to take our luggage. I was only too happy to off-load my pack but then we had to haggle the price before following after our porter as he deftly weaved in and out of the crowds with my heavy pack on his head. He led us through a tunnel under the tracks with stairs leading up to different platforms. We pushed through the crowds trying not to lose sight of our porter. Eventually he climbed the stairs to the appropriate platform and pointed us to our train. After tipping him, we walked down the length of the train, jostling shoulders with fellow passengers, looking for our names on the outside of the carriages. Finally we struggled aboard with our luggage amid quizzical stares of other passengers. We jammed our luggage under the seat.

Hopeful merchants immediately started pushing trays of food and trinkets through the windows asking for rupees. Shortly after we pulled out of the station, the family sharing our compartment took out their metal containers of chapatti and curried vegetables and laying out a cloth, spread out their food and started eating. They suggested we get out our food too. We just had some biscuits and bananas, not knowing what else was safe to eat. Chai wallas wandered through the train yelling chai, chai, coffee, coffee. Others came wanting to polish our shoes but we were only wearing sandals. Others crawled on the floor picking up bits of litter, also with their hands out for rupees.

Our fellow passengers showed us how to convert the seat to a tier of three bunks. The back-rest of the lower bench lifts up to form a middle bunk and is secured by straps to the bunk above. The next challenge was staggering down the corridor to the toilet. It was a little unnerving to see the tracks hurtling by underneath while squatting over the ceramic hole in the floor.

I settled down for the night, making sure the luggage was secure, then crawled into my sleeping sheet and pulled my camp pillow under my head. Several passengers secured their luggage to the lower bunk with a chain attached to rings suspended underneath the bunk.

The steady rhythm of the train soothed me to sleep but anxiety for the luggage and frequent stops denied a restful night. I had set the alarm as we were due to arrive at 5.30am. In the dark it was difficult to read the names of the stations especially when most of the signs were written in Hindi. Luckily other passengers ensured we got off at the right stop.

We disembarked at Raichur, stepping over sleeping bodies scattered on the platform. The Samuha jeep was there to meet us but we had to shake Pasha, the driver, awake as he was sleeping on the front seat with a blanket over his head. Then we began the long dusty drive to Jalahalli, which was to be my home for the coming year. I had survived my first few days in India, but barely. The best was yet to come.

3

ARRIVAL AT SAMUHA:

"Suffering cheerfully endured, ceases to be suffering and is transmuted into ineffable joy" Mahatma Gandhi

Jalahalli is a large sprawling village, two hours jeep drive from Raichur in Northern Karnataka. The only white people it has seen are the few English volunteers who have preceded me. We drove from Raichur through herds of goats and sheep and passed bullock carts, laden with people, slowly trotting along the tree-lined dusty roads.

Fields of cotton, corn, sugar-cane and sunflowers reached out towards the rocky landscape, interspersed with scattered villages. Groups of smiling children waved as we passed. When we met another jeep or a bus, it seemed like a game to see who could stay on the road longer before giving way to the oncoming traffic on the single lane road, horns blaring as we went.

At the entrance and exit to each village there were large speed bumps across the road to slow the vehicles down. If you hit them too fast, your head hit the roof in a hurry. It was an effective way of keeping the villages safe for the local villagers and children wandering down the road and the chickens, which tended to dart across the road right in front of you.

As we arrived at the Samuha campus, dozens of smiling faces came out to greet us with glistening smiles and the customary folded hands of Namaskara. Namaskara is the

Kannadda language version of the Hindi, Namaste. This is a sign of respect with palms held together, fingers pointing up and a slight bowing of the head. This is the Indian equivalent of shaking hands. The greeting was accompanied by “Oota itu?” which means “have you eaten?” a significant question in these rural villages. I immediately felt at home as these friendly people excitedly welcomed us to their campus. It felt like a safe refuge after all the hustle and bustle of Bangalore and the long train journey.

Samuha is an integrated rural development organisation in South India. The Community Based Rehabilitation program, or CBR, is just one component of it, which works with children with disability in rural villages and small towns in Northern Karnataka.

Venkoba, one of the Samuha staff, led us down the path, past a collection of thatched huts nestled under a canopy of trees to our house, a thatched mud hut with three concrete beds, a single naked light bulb and a hopeful looking fan. It was very hot here too and rivers of sweat were running down my body. I chose the bed by the open window, where I observed a pair of bullocks pulling a single wooden plough led by a dhoti clad farmer. A dhoti is the white home-spun cotton cloth wrapped around the loins in Gandhi style. I could look straight out from this bed on the passage of life which could only be India.

Sandra showed me the nearby bathroom, four walls surrounding a keyhole shaped ceramic hole in the ground and the inevitable trickling shower with a plastic bucket and jug. The roof was open to the sky and I grew to love this way of washing with the birds looking over you as the sun warms the water. This was April, the hottest month of the year so the temperature was still 47C. The first five days I was there, there was no electricity so no fans to cool us.

Two of the staff, Siddappa and Somanna, both skinny and clad in lungis, unloaded our luggage out of the jeep for us and carried it to our hut. A lungi is a wrap-around cloth tucked in at the waist and can be worn long to the ground but is mostly folded up at knee level and tucked into the waist for working.

My first task was to unpack then try out the "shower." Sandra showed me how to pour water into a bucket then use a plastic jug to pour the water over the body, soap down and rinse off with another jug of water. It is traditional to always shower before breakfast although there is no hot water then as the water is only heated by the sun beating down on the black water tank. It was a little unnerving to wash under the open sky but at least there were four walls to offer privacy. I changed into my new salwar kameez and felt refreshed, for at least a few minutes.

Next was nasta (breakfast) in the Mess where all the meals are cooked and eaten communally. Spicy aromas beckoned. Mudurangappa, the jovial cook, greeted me with a "Namaskara." Somanna, another cook greeted me shyly and Venkoba, smiled and said "Good Morning Madam" as he swept the floor with a short straw broom.

They showed me how to rinse off the metal plate then Mudurangappa ladled the food on to my plate.

Nasta consisted of uppitu, which is a savoury solid porridge made from millet. Eating utensils aren't used in rural India so I learnt how to eat this food with my fingers. I gingerly picked up a sticky piece of uppitu and put it in my mouth, in fact I later learnt to roll it into a ball then propel it into my mouth with a flick of the thumb. I sat down on the bench around the Mess where we sat cross-legged holding the plates on our lap. Eating in the Mess is a social time on campus but language was a challenge. All the senior staff could speak English and the disability workers had limited English but the cooks and other staff only spoke their own language, Kannada.

Samuha had a borewell so the water was clean and safe but I didn't trust it yet so I got pretty dehydrated those first few days. Somanna hauled the water from the well each morning in earthenware pots on a trailer behind his bicycle. He placed the pot in the shade with muslin cloth over the top to keep it cool. He placed a single metal cup on the pot and this was how we drank. Everyone shared this one cup but the cup never touched the lips. I got soaked a few times before I perfected this skill of pouring the water down my throat.

After breakfast Narayanswamy showed me around the campus and introduced me to the staff. Narayanswamy was the head of the disability sector and we were to work closely together to develop the program and to provide education to the village-based disability workers. He wore western style clothes with a cotton shirt, sleeves rolled up to the elbows, and loose cotton pants and sandals. He must have been about 30 years old with a mop of black hair swept across his forehead and one of the few men without a moustache. He was fluent in English and gentle in his manner.

The campus comprised a collection of thatched mud and wattle huts, where the staff lived. Our hut was directly opposite the disability centre, a large thatched building with a set of parallel bars outside. The whole campus was shaded by trees and purple bougainvillea sprawled over the rooves of the buildings.

Not far from our hut was the four walled bathroom. Next to that was the Mess where we all ate. The food was cooked over an open wood fire. Opposite the Mess was Pradeep's house and compound. Pradeep was the founder of Samuha, an organization working with the poorest of the poor in the state of Karnataka in South India. Pradeep was in charge of all the programs including dry land horticulture, animal husbandry, health, education, sanitation and micro-credit but Narayanswamy had free rein over the disability sector. Pradeep also had excellent command of English and a dynamic personality.

Past the Mess was the computer room. There Narayanswamy, introduced me to Mahesh, who was the computer guru.

"This is Hilary, a physiotherapist from Canada who is going to be with us for the next six months."

"Welcome to Samuha Hilary. If you need any help with the computers, just ask me."
"I've never used a computer before in my life," was my reply.
"What! Well, we'll have to change that. We do all our reports on the computer." He laughed.
"I thought I'd be able to get through life without having to learn how to use a computer at my age." I replied.
"Oh well. It's not so difficult. Between Narayanswamy and me, we'll teach you. We don't have a phone line here but we do have computers. The power often goes off but then we just start up the generator. This computer here is just for the CBR program. We'll get you started on it in a day or two."
"OK," I agreed.

Mahesh was on crutches since he had suffered from Guillaine Barre Syndrome, a neurological condition, and hadn't made a full recovery. He was taller than most of the staff, very friendly and welcoming and again had a great command of English. His hut was opposite ours, between the clinic and the bathroom. We were to have many social evenings around his hut. Beyond the computer room was Narayanswamy's hut and beyond that, accommodation for the female staff. For some reason western women were treated as if they were men in some situations so we were the only females living near the men's huts

After this tour, we walked back to the disability clinic. There was a line-up of children and their families waiting

outside laughing and chatting. First of all, Narayanswamy introduced me to the CBR staff.
Kallappa was the most senior disability worker, having been with Samuha the longest.
"Namaskara Madam."
Kallappa was quite short with thinning hair on top and wore a dhoti. He had a family and lived in a neighbouring village.
Ashok was the orthotic technician.
"Good Morning Madam. Welcome!"
He was the only one who had any formal training and had some English. He walked with a limp having had polio as a child. He kept his hand in his pocket and pushed back on his right thigh every time he bore weight on that leg in order to stabilize the knee.

Rangamma and Chandamma, with long braided hair and wearing saris, were the two female disability workers. Yellappa was the newest member of the team. He was a cobbler and his job was to make shoes for the braces that Ashok made for the children with polio. Yellappa had never been to school and was unable to read or write but he had a great memory.

"Namaskara everyone. My name is Hilary and I am looking forward to working with you." Narayanswamy translated this into Kannadda for the group.

My role was to teach physiotherapy to this small team of five village rehabilitation workers. Luckily I wasn't expected to start work that first day so I observed the interactions between the disability workers and the children and families. There was a large shaded area along the side of the disability centre where families sat on the ground and the staff examined the children and showed family members how to help them.

A set of parallel bars along the side of the building enabled a child to practice walking with a brace on his leg. Another young child had a cast on his leg down to his toes. A couple of babies were cradled by their mothers. The women pulled their saris over their heads in a sign of humility when I was introduced. The small children wore no underpants and when they peed, the mom just pulled the child to the edge of the compound and mopped up with the hem of her sari.

Before long, Venkoba brought a tray of tiny metal cups of chai. Everything stopped while we sipped the hot, spicy, sweet drink. Kallappa chatted and asked me my name and "how was my journey?" He told me how the child in the cast had a club foot and the boy in the parallel bars had polio which had caused paralysis in his leg. The babies in their Mother's arms also had polio but this was their first visit.

.

Ashok and Yellappa were working in the small workshop making a splint and shoe for the child with club foot. Rangamma and Chandamma interviewed the new mothers with their babies and told them how to position these babies with polio to prevent deformities and told them not to take them to the village doctor for injections at this stage as that trauma could actually cause paralysis of the muscles.

After spending time in the clinic, it was time for lunch or oota. This was ready any time after 1pm. It consisted of heapings of white rice with a thin tomato based vegetarian gruel, called sambar, and a spoonful of dall or chick-peas for protein. I watched the staff play with their rice as they mixed it in with the sambar and gathering it with their fingers, placed it in their mouths. I tried to copy this but inevitably some escaped back on to the plate. I learnt to pick the pieces of chilli out of the food in an attempt to decrease its extreme spiciness.

During the hot weather season, the team rested for a couple of hours in the afternoon or caught up on their paper work so I was glad to finish unpacking and settle into my new abode. I hadn't slept much on the train and in the extreme heat was feeling pretty lethargic. I lay out my sleeping sheet and installed the mosquito net over the concrete bed, which supported a one inch thin mattress.

After a couple of hours rest, Narayanswamy took me into the village of Jalahalli to meet Veenakumari. She was a young girl with cerebral palsy who lived with her family near the market. A long driveway led from the campus down to the road and a short walk across the field took you to the village of small shops, a temple, the bus station and a bustle of activity. I sat behind Narayanswamy on his motor-bike and we drove through the narrow streets between homes built from granite. Veenakumari lived with her Mother, Grandmother and siblings and she greeted us with a big smile. She was unable to walk and could only drag herself on her butt from one room to another. We decided that what she needed was a low wooden seat on wheels that she could manoeuvre herself around the home and a low commode that she could raise herself up onto for toileting and washing. Later we would make her a low table and bench for her to do her school work on. The family was happy with this plan and, after the customary cup of chai, we bade them farewell with plans to return the following week.

After this visit we returned to Samuha campus. Saried women walked along the road carrying large loads of fodder or firewood on their heads. Men and boys herded sheep and goats down the road and a bullock cart, led by a pair of Brahma bullocks, trundled by with several villagers on board. Pink hibiscus grew along the side of the road, enhancing this pastoral scene. Smells of farming, such as harvested grains and dung, mingled with the dust flying off the road and the sound of bells on the bullocks' necks filled the air.

Once we reached campus and freshened up from the hot and dusty drive, it was time for supper. The evening meal was ready around 8pm and again consisted of rice and sambar. All of these meals contained red hot chillis and were extremely spicy. By now I was exhausted from the long day and all the sights and sounds of rural India. I was hot and dusty so had a bucket shower from the sun-warmed water. I settled on to the hard concrete bed but it was too hot to pull down the mosquito net.

I fell asleep immediately but later woke to the feeling of fur brushing past my face. I fearfully grabbed the mosquito net and pulled it down hurriedly and secured it under the mattress so nothing could reach me in the bed. I presumed it must have been a rat but a couple of weeks later, I saw a cat take that same route. I never slept without the mosquito net around me after that, as it gave a great sense of security from all kinds of unwelcome creatures.

4
2nd Day in Jalahalli:

"There is more to life than simply increasing its speed"
Mahatma Gandhi

We woke at 6am and some families were already trickling into the clinic. The day started early with a small cup of chai followed by a cold bucket shower before setting out for the villages by motor-bike with Narayanswamy and Kallappa. Sandra, the nurse and my hut companion, worked in the health program, whereas I worked in the disability program so we didn't see much of each other except in the morning and evening.

The drive involved wending over dusty narrow trails to reach the client's house, in the middle of fields. This grew to be my favourite part of the day. Villages of straw and mud huts nestled into the reddish hillsides. Wisps of smoke curled up lazily against the rising sun. Barefoot villagers walked down the road carrying their food and tools on their heads as herds of goats, sheep and buffalo wandered towards their grazing grounds. We started the day early so that we could catch families at home before they departed for their field work.

We visited two houses that morning to provide therapy to the children with polio and to advise the parents. We were greeted with the customary "Namaskara" and invited into their homes and provided with more sweet cups of milky tea. Most of the homes were built with a wood frame with walls made of mud and a bamboo and thatch straw roof. The animals, buffalo, goats and bullocks lived in the lower portion of the house with the family living area raised up on a platform. They cooked on a wood fire in a corner of the home.

Most houses in the villages didn't have bathrooms or running water so toileting was done down the road or in a nearby field. Water was hauled from a well and a bucket and jug style shower was performed outside. Nearly every house had a shaded patio area where we did our treatments. The mother laid out a blanket on the stone deck and, having slipped off our sandals, we climbed up on to the platform and sat cross-legged while the child was washed and set down in front of us on the blanket. Family members sat around and in no time half the village crammed forward around us to see the strange white person in their midst. Despite my Indian clothing, I still looked very strange to them.

Arun was a young boy with club foot. Kallappa attempted to correct the foot but it was very tight. He taught the mother how to do stretching exercises then we asked them to bring him to the clinic the next day so we could apply plaster after stretching the foot towards a more normal position. The family agreed to do this and were willing to pay the cost of the plaster bandage.

The next child, in the same village, was Devappa, a young boy with polio. He wasn't able to straighten his right knee or hip. They were both stuck at about 90 degrees and only with strong pressure could the limb be stretched and straightened a few degrees. The mother had been taught how to do this and this time Kallappa had plaster with him to make a cast to hold the knee in the stretched position. The mother poured some water into a bucket. Narayanswamy and I held the leg as straight as we could to stretch it while Kallappa applied the plaster from thigh to ankle. We did this with the child lying down on his back to straighten the knee as much as possible. Devappa was then asked to sit up so that he got even more stretch behind the knee. Mom was also taught to lay him on his stomach for an hour daily with a sand-bag on his buttocks to stretch the front of the hip. This was to be repeated daily and on Kallappa's next visit he would remove the plaster, stretch the knee some more and re-apply plaster in the newly stretched position. This process would be repeated until the knee and hip were straightened or until we couldn't gain any more range. Devappa would then be fitted with a caliper, if the knee was corrected, otherwise he would be sent for corrective surgery in Bangalore.

After these visits we returned to campus on our bikes in time for a hot, spicy breakfast. This was followed by some paper work to keep the records up to date and preparation of some teaching notes on measuring joints and assessing muscle strength. Once I settled into the routine, we also made use of this time for some practical review and teaching.

Lunch consisted of piles of rice, a scoop of lentils and the thin spicy vegetarian sambar. After a rest, we headed out again to the villages to see some more clients in their homes after they had returned from their field work. The most extreme heat slightly dissipated after 3pm, which was a more acceptable time to venture out again under the sun.

The landscape in the Deccan Plateau of South India is remarkable for its rocks. It looks as though a series of massive explosions must have taken place as huge rocks pile on top of each other at impossible angles. Some rocks are simply split along fault lines whereas others are balanced on top of each other haphazardly. These rocks are red, as is the soil. In fact large rocks are dug up from beneath the soil for use in building and house construction. These red rocks are mostly basalt but there is also a large amount of granite which is a valuable commodity and largely exported.

The history of the Deccan Plateau features a vast volcanic eruption over sixty five million years ago which continued for thousands of years. This must be the source of these large volcanic basalt hills. Villages nestle into these rocky outcrops and monkeys can be seen perched on the rocks. Bears also make their home there although the only bears we saw were tame ones on a chain, used for entertainment. These bears are sloth bears.

The Deccan Plateau comprises the Southern peninsular of India being bound by the coastal mountain ranges, known as the Western and Eastern Ghats. These ranges come together at the Southern tip of India. The plateau is mostly arid but some large rivers do flow through from the Ghats. The coastal strips are fertile and lush with coconut plantations, fruit trees, rice paddy and sugar cane.

Fields of bright yellow sunflowers greeted us as we travelled the dirt roads on our motor bikes. The whole field of large yellow blooms faced the eastern sun in unison in the morning. By noon the heads turned up towards the overhead sun and as evening falls, the heads droop towards the ground until the sun shows its face again in the morning. Sunflowers are grown here for their oil. The heads are harvested after they have turned brown and drooped. The seeds are then removed and dried before being milled and the oil extracted. The stalks are fed to the cattle.

There were also fields of cotton. This valuable crop grows as shrubs with their distinctive fluffy balls nestling amongst their leaves. Chillis and lentils are grown in quantity and the chillis provide colour when they are spread out to dry in the sun. Onions and tomatoes are also plentiful and tall coconut palms provide shade for the crops. Millet is the staple food and is ground to flour for rotis, a flat bread. Wheat is also grown and used for chapattis. Corn is grown not only for the kernels, which are mostly ground into cornmeal, but also after the kernels have been harvested, the cobs are collected in a large pile and mixed with dung to be used as fuel. None of the plant is wasted as the leaves and stalks are fed to the cattle. Dung is collected daily and formed into patties and dried in the sun for fuel for cooking.

Trees grow fast here and apart from the palms, they include eucalyptus, mimosa, tamarind and many other varieties but the most revered is the neem tree. These trees are considered sacred and a stone platform is built around the base as a gathering place for villagers. The neem tree has potent medicinal properties. The leaves can be ground down to a paste, which is used for skin conditions including burn treatment. The stems are used to make chutney and can be taken medicinally for stomach and flu like ailments. There are also a variety of fruit trees such as banana, papaya, pomegranate and mango. It is also common to see fields of water melons as we drive by.

At the end of the day, we returned again to campus for spicy vegetarian dinner followed by camaraderie and building of friendships, outside Mahesh's hut. Several of the Sector Heads of different programs of Samuha congregated here. I met Phani, in charge of micro-credit, Balakrishna, in charge of the health program and Elango, who helped with computers. They came from different parts of the State or even from neighbouring States so the language kept switching from Kannada to English to Tamil to Telegu. I asked them to converse in English so I could join in, which they did but they also loved talking in their own languages so sentences were a mixture of words from several languages but mostly I could get the gist of it.

There are thirteen official languages in India with English being one of them. They obviously enjoyed each other's company and there was much laughter and friendship. Mahesh and Narayanswamy seemed to tell the best stories but Phani was pretty funny too. I tore myself away from their warm companionship and retired to my bed under the mosquito net looking forward to more evenings of this warmth and friendship. I fell asleep as soon as my head hit the pillow, exhausted from all the new experiences of the day and anxiously anticipated the days ahead.

5
Motor-bike and Community Based Rehabilitation:

"I just wish people would realise that anything is possible if you try; dreams are made possible if you try"

Terry Fox

The next day I had my first lesson on the motor-bike. Syed, one of the mechanics, taught me. Apart from my disastrous one attempt in England, I had never ridden a motor-bike except as a pillion the last few days with Narayanswamy. The bike that was to be mine was more like a trail-bike. It was called a TVS. It had no gears and its maximum speed was 40km/hr. First of all Syed showed me how to start it, how to accelerate and how to apply the brakes. I sat behind him for the first two lessons – just along the campus driveway - then I was allowed to drive it myself while he rode along-side on his own bike. Once they thought I had learnt the ropes, Narayanswamy took me into Raichur to take my driver's test. I had only to pay some money, answer a few questions, provide my photograph and I was away.

To begin with I was nervous on the narrow roads but gradually I learnt to love this new mode of transport. The biggest problem was that the lights got brighter the faster you drove so when I was going slow on the sandy, rocky trails at night, I could barely see as the lights were so dim. Once the rains came in June, it was also a difficult time to drive on the rutted soft trails.

For the first few weeks, I either went with Narayanswamy on his bike or else went on my TVS behind one of the other disability workers' bikes. This is mostly how we travelled except to some of the nearer villages where I had no trouble finding my way and language wouldn't be a problem. The disability workers had picked up quite a bit of English so they were the interpreters in the village between me and the families. Narayanswamy was the translator between me and the disability workers for training sessions, when it was important that they got a good grasp of the information and there was no lack of understanding.

The weekly pattern for Samuha's Community Based Rehabilitation, CBR, program consisted of home visits from Monday to Thursday with one hour of practice or teaching in the evenings. On Fridays we had assessment clinics, where families brought their children for assessment. These were the busiest days. The families came without appointments and started congregating around 6am at the clinic. We kept going without stopping until the last family had been seen, often around 6pm. We snatched a tea and some food whenever the opportunity arose. Nearly all the children that came to these clinics were children with polio and a few with club-feet. Word spread throughout the villages that these rehabilitation services were available in Jalahalli and families flocked there for help.

Saturdays were dedicated to training. The disability workers were expected to teach back the previous week's lesson. I then taught new material such as anatomy, how to perform resisted exercises, how to measure muscle strength and joint range as well as numerous other topics. The rest of the day we spent practicing on each other to make sure that the material was all well understood.

Sundays were meant to be free but we often did awareness programs in the villages on Sunday evenings. These awareness programs consisted of puppet shows, slide-shows and songs all about the importance of hygiene, immunisations and inclusive education. Several of the children with disability participated in these events and the CBR team co-ordinated the program. These programs were performed monthly in different villages and always caused excitement and anticipation in the village. The puppet shows were brilliantly done and somehow Ashok managed to get his puppet to smoke and you'd see the smoke rising out of the puppet's mouth and then he'd start vomiting. Of course this brought gales of laughter from the audience!

Most of the villages had no electricity so we always brought a generator with us. When we first arrived at the village, only the men turned up for the show but Samuha insisted that the women should be there too. The staff went door to door encouraging the women and children to come out, which they did. According to local culture the women always sat in one group and the men in another. These shows were performed outside where everyone sat on the ground and we erected a small stage for the puppet show and a large screen for the slides. Everyone enjoyed these events but they also provided important messages regarding health and education. It was important that the women be included as they then taught the rest of the family.

One time, we were putting on an awareness program in the nearby village of Kardigudda. As the rest of the team were getting the generator and stage organized, I climbed up on to the stone platform that surrounded a large neem tree. Immediately one of the men sitting there started yelling at me but of course I couldn't understand a word he said. Narayanswamy hurried over and spoke to the man in Kannada and asked me to step down on to the ground. After a while the man calmed down and stopped yelling.

"What was that all about?" I asked Narayanswamy.

"Neem trees are sacred and you can't stand on the platform with your shoes on as it desecrates its sanctity. It's alright, I explained that you didn't know the culture and he accepted that."

"I'm sorry" I replied. "I won't do that again!"

Who knew? Culture can be so sensitive.

Also, once a month on a Sunday, we held an orthopedic clinic in Raichur with the orthopedic surgeon there to help diagnose and refer our more complicated clients. I found it amazing that no-one complained about these long hours but the staff were all dedicated to improving the lives of these children.

I took advantage of these monthly trips to Raichur to phone home. Communication was difficult as internet and email were not yet available. I wrote letters but they took at least a week in each direction. There was only a local phone in Jalahalli, so in order to phone home, I had to get someone to drive me the two hours to Raichur to a pay phone. Cell phones were not yet available, so if Floyd wasn't at home when I rang, all I could do was leave a short message. He had no way to return my call. For the most part this was fine as I had so much to occupy my mind with new adventures and experiences but when important decisions had to be made, it was difficult, as we found out later.

Family is all important in India. Young children look after their siblings while their parents work in the field. The grand-parents contribute to the well-being of the family and the three generations live together under one roof. Growing and preparing food is the main daily occupation.

Children go to school if they are not needed to help out in the field or in the home. Another reason for a low literacy rate is the practice of bonded labour. Villagers become indebted to the landlord. They have no way of paying back their loan so instead they bond their children to the landlord to work his fields in repayment for their loan. This becomes a vicious cycle which is passed on through generations, limiting the ability for children to gain an education. The literacy rate in 1994 was only 11% in these villages.

Disability is a huge hardship on the family as everyone is expected to contribute to the welfare of the family. It is our job, as disability workers, to reduce the disability and to provide income generation programs along with vocational training and to facilitate education. Therapy is always designed to enhance ability rather than just to strengthen a muscle or limb.

My motor bike skills came in handy when we were asked to see Prabhu in a remote hut. Prabhu was six years old when I met him. He had TB of the spine. He had just returned from Bangalore where the surgeon removed the infected bone and tissue and fused his vertebrae. Prabhu was in a full body cast for six weeks to allow the spine to heal properly. During this time he needed daily injections of antibiotics to ensure there was no further infection. He also had to continue with the TB medicines for two years. The family lived 15 kms off the road along a dusty dirt track then across some waste fields scattered with thorns. They lived in a small hut made of mud walls with the typical long thatch roof with a thorn hedge around three sides. There were no trees for shelter but the goats had a wicker basket- weave shelter and the skinny buffalo just found shade where it could. There was no water in sight.

Their hut was on its own outside the village of Medinapur and it was very dry and barren land. They grew some ground nuts, onions and millet as these grow well there in spite of the severe droughts. Prabhu's mother was small and frail with wispy grey hair. She had another younger son living with her too but the father was nowhere to be seen.

The main problem was that Prabhu needed these daily injections to survive. The house wasn't accessible by jeep and was too far away to walk. The English nurse Sandra, who was staying with Samuha, had never ridden a motorbike. I had never given intra-muscular injections but I knew how to give subcutaneous injections, as my grandson has had diabetes since he was two years old and needs twice daily injections but this was different. There were more serious consequences if you did it wrong like a huge abscess developing from unsterile technique. I loved riding the motor-bike and Sandra showed me how to give the injection using a precious orange for practice. I took on the challenge.

The first time I went with Kallappa, one of the disability workers. He explained to the family what needed to be done and I think I managed to hide my nervousness from the family. It helped that Prabhu was brave and hardly cried. Kallappa came with me a couple of times and after that I started going on my own. Although we couldn't speak each other's languages, we managed. I had to be careful not to drive over any thorns as they were long and sharp enough to cause a puncture and then how would I get help? Fortunately this didn't happen.

Kallappa had an accident on his motorbike one day. He is very short and the bike was too big for him. I never felt safe when I was driving with him. This time he was alone when he hit a rough patch in the road and fell off. The bike fell on top of him, resulting in a big wound on his leg. Again he needed daily attention but he couldn't drive to Samuha so he asked if I would go to him each day and change his dressings. I agreed to do this thinking I would be able to show his wife what to do, but Kallappa would have none of this as he figured she wouldn't understand how to do it right.

I drove there daily on my own; it was on a dirt road all the way, about 12km from the campus. One day when I was still on the main road, I met two bikes whose drivers waved and spoke to me in English as they went by. I turned off the road shortly after that towards Kallappa's hut and to my dismay they doubled back and turned off the road behind me and soon caught up and started making conversation. I tried to ignore them but they were persistent. One kept alongside of me as the other one drove in front so I was forced to stop. I was pretty scared in this remote unpopulated area and these people were obviously not from around there as they were wearing western clothes and could speak English. They could see that I was nervous and thankfully they let me go. I continued on to Kallappa's. I couldn't tell Kallappa about the incident as his English wasn't good enough to understand but I told Pradeep once I got back to campus. He was alarmed but fortunately there were no further incidents, however I wasn't allowed to drive out on my own after that.

Every day brought surprises and new experiences. One day we passed two men on a motor bike carrying two live sheep between them. The sheep were held with their backs supported on the seat and their feet tied together, held by the pillion rider. Presumably they were heading for market.

Bullock carts were loaded down with huge loads of crops across their width, taking up most of the road, as the driver in front coaxed the pair of bullocks straining under the load. Villagers walk several kilometers between their home and their fields carrying their tools on their head. Some of them carry huge loads of hay on their heads so that all you can see is a pair of skinny legs under a moving hay stack. Others lead the cattle, goats and sheep out to the field every morning and back to the village each night. Everyone who is physically able has a job to contribute to the well-being of the family.

Obesity is rare in these villages and nutrition is barely enough to sustain the hard work necessary for life. The contrast between the way of life in these rural villages compared to the affluence of life in the west is humbling. The burden of disability, added to the poverty, is almost more than families can bear but they are still cheerful, generous and welcoming.

6
Polio

"You have to be the best you can be with what you have"
Rick Hansen (Man in Motion)

Siddappa was one of the first children affected by polio who sought help from Samuha. He was sitting with his family outside their hut when we drove down the tree-lined dirt track to his village, Hosur Siddappur. A few goats were tethered nearby and chickens strutted across the red earth. Siddappa was ten years old. He was the second son of a very poor family and his disability was a great blow to them as, apart from not being able to contribute to the welfare of the family, he was an added drain on their meagre resources.

He had been pulling himself on his belly through his village all his life. Both his legs were paralysed including his hips and low back but his arms were strong. His hips and knees were fixed in a frog position, unable to be straightened at all. Siddappa's main ambition was to get a wheel-chair so he could mobilize around his village.

Samuha had already taken him under their wing when I met him and had provided a long series of corrective surgeries and rehabilitation. Eventually his legs were straightened and he was fitted with long leg braces to support his hips and legs. When I met Siddappa, the family, with Samuha's guidance, had erected parallel bars for him to practice standing and walking outside his home. He couldn't believe that he could now look at people eye to eye and communicate with them without having to look up from the ground like a serpent. When he stood up in the parallel bars for the first time, his grin spread across his whole face.

After much practice he managed to balance on crutches and learnt to swing both his legs through, balance on two feet and move his crutches forwards. He would need to repeat this action many times in order to walk the five kilometers over rough ground to school each day to get an education. We chatted with the family and they agreed to send Siddappa to school, once he had mastered the crutches.

He later learnt how to make braces for other people with disability and joined the Samuha staff. He became an assistant to the orthotic technician. On World Disability day he stood up on stage with a mic, supported on his crutches, and sang and danced a popular rock song. When he got too carried away with the rhythm, he lost his balance and fell to the ground, so his friends just lifted him back up and he carried on, not missing a beat!

On this first visit to India, polio was still endemic as although the vaccine was available, it had to be kept cooler than 4 degrees Celsius to remain potent. Since most of these villages had no electricity and temperatures could reach as high as 47 degrees Celsius, children were contracting the polio virus in spite of receiving the impotent vaccine. We saw thirty new cases in the local villages that summer. When this happened, it took much convincing to encourage other families to bring their children for immunization.

The majority of the clients we saw were children afflicted by polio as well as some with club foot and a few with cerebral palsy. Polio is a debilitating disease caused by a virus that attacks the spinal cord, leading to paralysis of affected muscles. Only one percent of people infected by the virus develop paralysis and by the time children reach two years of age in rural India, if they have not already been paralysed by polio, they are considered to have developed immunity to the disease. The affected muscles become paralysed but other muscles remain strong so gross deformities develop. Often children have had polio for several years before they receive any treatment so they have severe deformities, mostly of the legs, from crawling on their knees for years, unable to walk.

Rehabilitation consists of teaching the parents stretching exercises followed by serial casting to correct the deformity. Once the limbs have been straightened, they are fitted with braces. Then comes the exciting process of teaching them to walk for the first time. The smiles on their faces when they stand upright for the first time and take their first tentative steps are precious. The more severe cases require surgery to correct the deformities but most of the work can be done in the village. After this process they are able to walk to school with the aid of braces and crutches. Now they have a chance in life.

In those early days, when we put on awareness programs in the villages to teach the importance of going to school, especially for children with disability, there was only eleven percent literacy in these villages but when children have a disability it is crucial that they become educated as they are not able to do the field work to support themselves so need to learn other skills.

Lakshman often featured in these awareness programs. He had polio that affected one of his legs and was fitted with a caliper and crutches. He was then able to walk to school and get an education, which helped him later find work in his village.

Another young boy was Virupakshi. He was four years old when his parents brought him to our campus for assessment. He had suffered with a fever and was unable to move his left leg. His right leg was also weak. We showed the family how to do exercises to correct the deformity in his knee, hip and ankle joints. He presented as typical polio in his legs. This also caused him to have a short left leg. We needed to do serial casting to correct his deformities so we straightened his knee through stretching exercises, as much as we could, and applied a cast. This procedure was repeated every two weeks until his knee was straight then Ashok, the orthotic technician, measured him for a shoe raise as well as a caliper. First the family built a set of parallel bars outside his house so he could practice walking and then he progressed to crutches. When he was old enough, he attended school. He also joined the awareness program group. He went on to perform street theatre and became part of the organization of people with disabilities. Later he joined the disability team and worked with children who had a hearing impairment.

Another day we visited a Lambani Village. These are tribal people who dress differently and have their own language and customs. The women are very colorful with rings through their nose and ears and they wear bright red dresses covered with small mirrors. The Lambani are famous for their dancing and singing. We met a young boy there called Dakoji. He had polio in both his legs and he moved around his village on his haunches by pulling each foot forward with his hands – a slow laborious process. He had severe contractures in his hips and knees so his grand-father agreed to let Samuha take him to Bangalore for corrective surgery. After this he needed bilateral calipers and crutches but he was delighted to be able to walk upright. He progressed to one caliper and two crutches, then one caliper and one crutch and now he just needs one caliper.

Unfortunately a disability is a great handicap for a girl in India when it comes to marriage. It greatly reduces her chances and if she can't marry, how can she support herself? Sometimes the family marries the girl to the Temple and she becomes a Devadasi. The Devadasi system is a religious practice in parts of southern India, whereby parents marry a daughter to a deity or a temple. The marriage usually occurs before the girl reaches puberty and requires the girl to become a prostitute for upper-caste community members. They are forbidden to enter into a real marriage. This practice is now abandoned by law but the practice does still exist amongst particular castes.

One young girl, Ayyamma, came to us from a distant village when she was ten years old with a severe club foot. She was able to walk with a marked limp but her foot was folded under her so that she walked on the outside ankle bone. This disability was reducing her chances of a good marriage. She was willing to attend the clinic every two weeks for stretching exercises and serial casting to correct this deformity. After one year the deformity was corrected sufficiently to enable a splint to be fitted to maintain the correction.

Sometimes we organized a field trip, usually to a Temple. This involved packing as many children and staff as we could into the jeep and preparing enough food for the day. The Samuha jeep collected the children and they stayed overnight so we could leave campus at 4am. It took some ingenuity to squeeze as many as fourteen of us into the jeep, some with crutches. All of these trips were memorable. Excitement and anticipation filled the canvas covered jeep. The children often sang songs as we travelled.

Roads were narrow and usually there was only room for one vehicle on the tarmac so when we met a truck or bus, at least one set of wheels had to drop down on to the shoulder. The destination was usually at least three hours away so we were happy to tumble out once we arrived.

One day I treated everyone to a pop. The surprise on Siddappa's face was priceless as he felt the bubbles burst inside his mouth. He was twelve years old but had never had a pop before. This is typical of most children in rural India. The laughter and excitement proved that money has nothing to do with happiness. None of these children had any toys. They all had a disability and some only had one set of clothes and yet their happiness was pure and infectious.

Elephant Stables Hampi

We wandered around the Temple, visited the elephant stables and enjoyed a substantial picnic before heading back to campus, arriving back well after dark. Before entering a Temple, one must remove ones footwear so as not to desecrate the sanctity of the Temple. The sad thing is that many people with polio who need braces have leather shoes fitted to the brace. This means that they can't enter the Temple unless they remove their braces, which is a laborious task and then they can only crawl around on their paralysed legs. These field trips however are the highlights of the year and many memories are indelibly printed on the psyche. One girl with polio of one leg, who used to come on these trips, was eleven year old Bharathi. Samuha made her a caliper and crutches and this pretty girl was able to walk easily with these assists.

Pulse polio day is a day when every child under five years old is immunized against polio. I participated in this a few times and it was always bliss to travel by motor bike through back roads and tranquil villages. When we arrived at one particular village, we went door to door to all 210 houses and ensured that all the children, 104 of them, received their immunization. This process is repeated twice annually throughout India until polio is eradicated in the country, which it now is but pulse polio is continued annually until neighbouring countries are also polio-free.

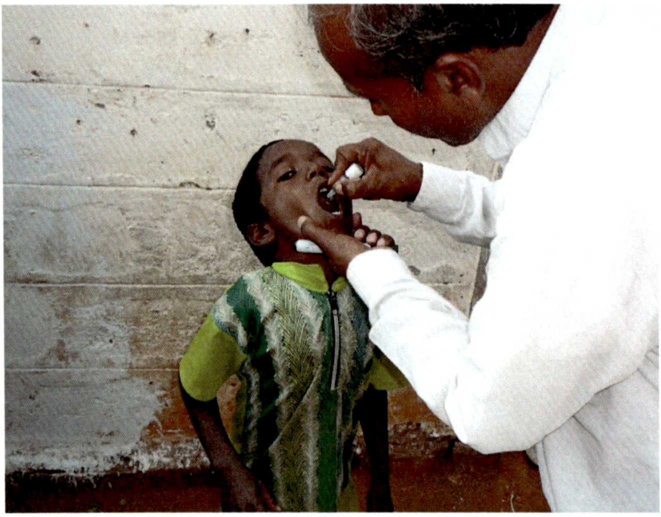

Polio vaccine

Since the vaccine is given by mouth and is sweet, the children were co-operative and we were followed by a happy throng as we proceeded from house to house. This village, we were visiting, was picturesque with banana trees and flowering shrubs and freshly swept red earth around each house. Most houses sheltered a herd of goats in a mesh pen in front of the dwelling and several herds were ushered through the village to find pasture. Bullocks with gaily painted horns lay placidly in pairs nearby. Chickens darted from place to place while docile dogs observed the scene. There was even a pair of bright green parrots perched up on the temple roof and a troupe of large grey monkeys passed through, swinging from tree to tree. Many houses were brightly painted with pictures of Gods or animals on the white and brown plastered walls.

During the course of the day we were invited into several houses for breakfast, lunch and numerous cups of tea. People here have very little and yet are so generous with their hospitality. Some houses were locked up because the families had uprooted to try and find work to support themselves. This area was undergoing severe drought as the rains were negligible. Most villagers work on the land and when crops fail, they have no other source of income or food so are in dire straits.

The children ran around happily with ragged shirts and little else. The women wore brightly coloured saris while some men wore western clothes but most wore the traditional home spun white dhoti wrapped around their lower body with a long shirt. Travelling by bike shortly after sunrise, we observed workers already out in the fields working their crops manually. One child scooped out dirt with half a coconut shell helping his father install a post for the clothes line. Men dug holes with hand-made shovels in preparation for new hydro poles. One old man sat cross-legged on the red dirt road opposite another elderly man who squatted on his haunches. He must have been the barber as he was shaving the other man with a straight edged blade.

Some children rolled a bicycle wheel with a stick while another child played with a stone inside a small cardboard box. Store toys were unknown here. A baby was cradled in a sari hung from a tree while the parents worked in the field below. Everyone smiled and waved and tried to engage in conversation. This pastoral scene of hard work and happiness is proof that money, beyond ones basic needs, is not necessarily the route to happiness. However, one does need a cushion to protect against abject poverty, which can be dire and a threat to life, as evidenced by the families who had to leave the village to find work to sustain themselves.

7
EXPANSION OF PROGRAM:

"If you think you are too small to make a difference try sleeping with a mosquito" H. H. Dalai Lama

Gradually we decided to expand the CBR program to provide services to the increasing number of children with polio and other ailments which required our services. We made home visits to any villages within a 60 km radius of the centre. Any further than that, the families had to come to us. We needed to expand the number of disability workers so we hired three more from the local villages. Ayyalappa, who was already on staff with Samuha as a teacher and who had carpentry skills, joined the team. Then Babumiya and Malakarjuna joined. Gradually more joined until we had a complement of twelve including two orthotic technicians.

Ayyalappa was from the village of Nilavangi where he did agriculture and carpentry. His carpentry skills came in very useful for building special seats, crutches, parallel bars and swings as well as building blocks and other toys for the children. Ayyalappa and Kallappa were very traditional villagers who always wore their dhoti in classic Gandhi style whereas most of the other male staff wore western pants and shirts. All of them wore sandals.

Babumiya was from a village near Deodurg, the closest small town to Jalahalli and about halfway between it and the city of Raichur. He also joined Samuha as a teacher in 1992 but joined the CBR program in 1994. He was also an agriculturalist and his home was surrounded by fields. Babumiya already supported a young family, when he joined the team. He was a quiet and industrious student, dedicated to his work. In 1995, he met with an unfortunate accident but that story will be related later. Malakarjuna was a village chief, or Gowda, He joined the same time as Babumiya. He was very funny, not so much through sense of humour, but rather through mannerisms and difficulties in comprehension of rehabilitation tasks. Malakarjuna generously provided many laughs during our training sessions.

One day someone from Jalahalli came to ask for help from Samuha. Chandamma, one of our disability workers who lived in Jalahalli, had been bitten by a snake in her home in the village. Mohinuddin, the store-man, took me on his motor-bike to Chandamma's house. The story was that she had gone down to the basement of her house in the dark. She hadn't seen the snake but she had a tell-tale fang mark on her foot and she was losing consciousness.

It was obvious that she needed immediate medical attention. Mohinuddin carried her out to his bike. I got on the bike behind Mohinuddin holding on tight to Chandamma, squeezed between us, as he drove to the Jalahalli hospital. She was losing consciousness fast. When we got to the hospital, we carried her in between us and explained the emergency to the doctor. We hadn't seen the snake so couldn't identify it so they gave Chandamma an injection of anti-histamine and instructed us to keep her awake overnight.

After a short rest, we took her back to campus on the bike, still holding on tight with her sandwiched between us. I asked Rangamma to stay with her in the hut to make sure she was ok overnight. She gradually recovered and by morning she was fine.

Rangamma, the other female disability worker, had had a tough life. She had been abused and abandoned by her husband and had a daughter to raise. One day she said she was tired and asked if she could lie down on my bed. I said, "of course" and she had a nap. She had long thick dark hair, as most of the girls do. Over the next few days, I noticed my scalp was itchy and Chandamma told me one morning there was something crawling down my neck. I had the dreaded lice! It seems it's quite common there and you often see Mothers combing their children's hair and picking out the nits. Chandamma told me what to do and took me shopping to get the medicated shampoo and a nit comb. I stripped the bed and put the thin mattress and pillow out in the direct sun to kill the bugs. After a few days the itchiness disappeared but it was a horrid feeling to know you had lice or nits!

I am used to taking daily walks and found that I wasn't getting enough exercise on campus as I spent most of my time either sitting on the ground, riding a motor-bike or riding in the jeep. On days that didn't require an early start, I decided to go for a short walk before breakfast. Mostly I walked down the driveway to the street, turned left away from the village and walked the narrow road towards the hills. I noticed there were nearly always men lining the road with small metal jugs in their hand. I idly wondered what they were doing but didn't pay much attention. Their purpose was later revealed. I walked for about half an hour then came back along the same route, by which time the men had usually disappeared.

I enjoyed this walk as the road was lined with pink hibiscus and there were often one or two men out in the red earth fields steering a single wooden plough, pulled by a pair of oxen. It amazed me how straight the furrows were. The man mostly stood on the plough or else walked along side it while holding the reigns of the oxen and gently steering them. It looked as though the oxen knew exactly what they were doing and where to go.

On Saturdays I walked further, along this same route then up the rocky hill, which stood sentinel over our campus. I preferred to take that walk with a companion as it was quite wild. There were stories of bears living up there but I never saw any sign of one. There was another big rocky hill further away from this campus where a hermit lived naked in a small temple. I never ventured there on my own. It took about an hour to climb up to the top of the rocks but then there was an expansive view over the surrounding peaceful landscape of fields, rocks, trees and thatched rooves. Usually you could hear farm sounds of roosters crowing and lambs bleating and occasionally donkeys braying. Always the birds were chirping and I loved hearing the mournful call of the doves.

One time when I took my morning walk down the road, some of the men were squatting alongside. I looked at the hibiscus and not at them as I hurried by. It was suddenly dawning on me what these men might be doing with their metal jugs. Later in the evening sitting around Mahesh's hut, Narayanswamy asked me,

"Where do you go on your morning walks?"

"Usually I turn left out the gate and walk down the road towards Hosur Siddappa," I replied.

The guys looked at each other and smiled.

Narayanswamy suggested, "Maybe you should take a different route another time or go at a different time of day."

"Is that where they go to the toilet every morning?" I naively asked.

"Yes," was the answer.

"Where do the women go?"

"They go in the fields. Later on the pigs come and clean it all up."

"Oh," I said. "I guess I'll just have to take a longer walk on the week-ends, after they've all finished their business."

"That's probably a better idea." They agreed.

Another enjoyable walk was across the field into the village. We often did this during the hot weather to get a cold mango juice from a village shop, which had a fridge. It was such a treat but by the time we had returned to campus, we were already thirsty again. When we walked across the field, we were always followed by excited groups of children saying "Hello Auntie" and "Photo, photo." They often wanted to hold our hands.

I had arrived in April, and April and May are the hottest months of the year until the rains come in June. As soon as the first downpour starts, everyone rushes out to get soaked in it. It is such a relief after the dry intense heat and after that the temperature gradually drops. June is a difficult month for travel but the farmers and everyone else are so happy to get the rains. In this drought prone area of the Deccan plateau, the rains fail about every third year. Then the crops fail and villagers have to migrate to the cities to try and find work in order to eat and survive.

One day Ayyalappa and I were traveling from Samuha to Arakera which was 40 km away. While we were driving in a remote hilly area, our tire was punctured and we had to push the bike back around 3 km to the nearest village. There was a garage in the village and they repaired the tire while we waited but it took a couple of hours to repair. This was the first time there had ever been a white woman in their village. Within no time there was a group of about twenty people circled around us and they just stared at me – very disconcerting but it seems to be customary as no-one seems to be at all bashful when they are caught staring, they just continue and may even start giggling. It was a relief to get away and be driven on rough roads through the hills in the picturesque but rocky countryside. We eventually reached Arakera, had lunch in an outdoor “restaurant” and did a couple of home visits before driving back to Jalahalli without incident.

The disability program has its own orthotic workshop, which is used for making all the aids and appliances, needed for people with disability. Ashok is the chief orthotic technician. He had polio when he was two years old affecting both of his legs but the right leg was much more affected. The muscles that straighten his knee and lift his foot up are completely paralysed and he only has minimal power in his hip muscles but he is still able to walk independently by pushing his right leg back with his hand every time he takes a step. In 1991 he trained for a year in Bangalore as an orthotic technician and set up the workshop in Jalahalli campus in 1992. In 2000 this workshop moved to Deodurg. Previously, in 1997, Ashok started an additional Samuha workshop in Raichur.

The workshops are used for making calipers, made out of pvc pipe, for children with polio. Also crutches, various splints and prosthetics or artificial limbs for amputees. Special seats and standing frames are also made in the workshop as Ayyalappa was needed for other work.

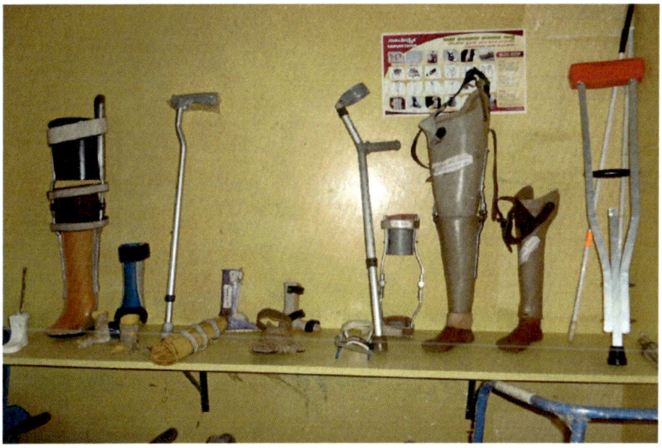

Some days we fitted young children with standing frames to enable them to start taking weight through their legs. Other children, with cerebral palsy, were fitted with special seats to give them support in sitting and to enable them to use their hands more effectively.

The calipers made of pvc pipe were much lighter than the usual metal ones, which were manufactured in Bangalore, so were much more suitable for children with polio in the villages. The prosthetics for amputees were quite rudimentary in the early days but gradually improved. People requiring upper limb prostheses still had to travel to Bangalore for their specialized needs.

In one village we saw three young boys, around ten years old, with polio. They were sitting on the ground happily playing marbles when they were called to their homes for lunch. They immediately turned on to all fours and speedily crawled down the street to their homes. Their hip and knee joints were fixed in severely flexed positions and most likely had been that way since they were two years old, as that was the most common age for these children to develop polio. They sped down the street and effortlessly climbed the steps up on to the patio of their home.

Although these children were happy and moving well, their future would be precarious as without an education, they would never be able to support themselves as adults. Samuha helped countless children like this by facilitating surgery to correct these severe deformities then provided the children with calipers and crutches. With home-made parallel bars installed outside the home, the children soon learnt to walk and quickly transitioned to crutches. Then they could go to school and become educated so they didn't need to rely on manual labour for their future.

- - - -

When I was working with people with back pain or arthritic knees in the Prince George Hospital, I kept thinking back to all the children with polio who had to crawl around their village and how their families spent every moment of their lives trying to grow enough food and earn enough cash to support their families. Our physiotherapy skills were so needed there to correct the deformities, make suitable splints and help the children get back on their feet and be able to walk again.

Mrs Smith was complaining of how her back hurt when she bent to lift the groceries out of her van. While I was mobilising her spine and teaching some strengthening exercises, my mind was thinking of Siddappa. How his legs had both been paralysed by polio but how he had persevered with his therapy and his impoverished family had managed to scrape enough funds together to get the required surgery to correct his deformities. They had overcome so much.

Many thoughts tumbled through my mind. "My skills are needed in rural India. The children there will be left to crawl around their village for the rest of their lives and eventually have to beg for food, if we don't help them in their recovery."

In the Prince George Hospital I continued to work with clients who were recovering from stroke, others who had received traumatic brain injuries and with clients with multiple sclerosis. All of these people needed physiotherapy to help them acquire their maximum function but I knew there was a choice of physiotherapists here who could help them. The children in India couldn't overcome their disability without skilled therapeutic interventions.

In India it was very difficult to find a physiotherapist, willing to leave the city to go to work in a rural backward part of India. There was the complication of caste and language too. Also Samuha couldn't afford to pay the full cost of a professional to provide these services. This is why they chose to train a team of local disability workers. Community Based Rehabilitation is a widely accepted form of providing needed therapy services to communities in poorer parts of the world such as in rural Asia and Africa. Queens University, in Kingston Ontario, pioneered this system and they host the Institution for Advancement of Community Based Rehabilitation, ICACBR. We extensively used their training manuals and advice for training Samuha's CBR team. Samuha relies on a foreign trained health professional, such as a physiotherapist, to volunteer their time to train their CBR team on an ongoing basis.

8
KERALA:

"Just one small positive thought in the morning can change your whole day" H.H. Dalai Lama

After five months in India, I was ready to take a vacation and wanted to go to Kerala. Kerala is on the south west coast of India and in the early nineties was still relatively unspoilt. I tried to talk Barbara, the English Doctor who came to Samuha at the same time as me, to go with me but she wasn't interested. I decided to book the trip anyway as I felt I should see more of India than just the project villages and Bangalore. I was nervous about going on my own as I wanted to go to the beach and travel the inland waterways but it's easier to do these things when accompanied.

Once I booked the trip, Barbara decided she'd like to come too after all, which was great. Once we had made this decision, we asked Samuha to make the reservations for us then we packed a small bag each and took leave from Samuha for a while. It was so much better to have a companion than to travel on one's own and fortunately we were both interested in seeing the same things. We reached Bangalore by train, then crossed over to the central bus station and took the bus to Mysore, about a four hour journey.

Mysore is a well-laid out city, the most impressive building being the palace. It dominates the city with its gothic style architecture. There are still royalty living there. The expansive building is largely made of granite with five pink marble domes. Inside, the rooms are spacious and many large paintings adorn the walls. At night it was beautifully lit up. The palace is particularly famous for its elephants and during the Dussehra Festival, people throng to see the parade of elephants decorated in their finery.

After visiting the palace, we took a bus to the famous bird sanctuary, home to many migratory birds including storks, ibis and herons. We also visited the Brindavan botanical gardens, which are famous for the colourful musical fountains as well as their large array of tropical plants. We found a good hotel for the night close to the palace, which looked magnificent with all the lights outlining every detail.

The next morning we took the bus to Bandipur National Park, south of Mysore. It is famous for its tigers but we never saw any. We did see elephants but some of them had chain marks round their ankles – do they have ankles? Anyway those ones obviously weren't wild. We went by jeep further into the jungle and saw several species of deer and some monkeys but no big game, apart from the elephants. We then spent the night in a hut in the park. Indian safaris are not nearly as glamorous as those in Africa.

The next day we continued south on to Ooty by bus. Unfortunately it was raining there but this is quite common as it is a hill station. We climbed steeply to reach the town which was surrounded by pine forest.

Ooty was a very popular escape for the British during the Raj, where they could enjoy the cool breezes in contrast to the stifling heat of the rest of India. We took the Nilgiri steam Mountain rack railway up the mountain and enjoyed breathtaking views of the terraced tea plantations on either side of the tracks. The train offered a wonderful vantage point of the valley below and surrounding lush vegetation.

From Ooty, we took the overnight train to Trivandrum on the Arabian Sea. Again it was raining and there was water running along the floor of the train so it was difficult to keep our luggage dry. The train crossed the Western Ghats to reach the coast. The Ghats are the mountain range that separate the Deccan Plateau from the coast. As soon as we were on the western side of the Ghats, the vegetation changed to dense rainforest. On the coast we saw lush fruit trees, citrus, coconut palms and cashew. Trivandrum is a large city situated on the coast but also on the backwaters of Kerala. We took an auto-rickshaw from the station to the pontoon on the inland waterway.

The Inland Waterways are like canals and are commonly called the Backwaters. The main arm runs parallel to the coast and we boarded a small passenger boat which took us for most of the day from Trivandrum to Cochin, another coastal town. Several fishing boats were moored at the dock and more were out fishing with their long nets suspended from poles arching up from the side of the boat. Houseboats also quietly plied the waters with their long wooden hulls and palm fringed rooves. Palm trees lined the shores and many settlements nestled into the shade of the trees. Every part of the palm tree is used. The wood from the trunk is used for building, the palms are used for roofing and the coconut husks are used for matting and woven into awnings to shelter both people and animals. It was a gloriously colourful sight as we slowly cruised along the calm water.

Mangroves lined the shore in places. Many birds flittered about and rice paddy and banana plantations also lined the route. All the boats were slow paced and quiet although most were under power. It was a most peaceful journey as we drank in the sights of calm existence along the shore as families wove their mats, built their boats, fished and generally went about their daily chores in these idyllic villages.

Once we reached Cochin, we took a bus to Kovalom and from the bus station took a taxi to the beach and hotel region. We hadn't booked a hotel but we asked the driver if he knew of a small hotel on the beach. He was delighted to show us one and led us across rice paddy as there was no street access to it This was quite an adventure as we walked through extensive paddy, along their banks, before we reached the beach. Set back a little way from the Arabian Sea but still virtually on the beach was our small hotel. The driver must have got a commission for taking us there as otherwise no-one would know that it existed but we were thankful for his trouble.

We were shown to our tiled room with two single beds in it and a sea-view through the open window. The proprietor showed us the bathroom and explained to us that when we wanted a shower, she would heat up a bucket of water for us. Although simpler than we expected, this plan worked out perfectly. We were in an idyllic setting and there were no other tourists around. It was like arriving in a little piece of Heaven.

We immediately dropped our luggage and walked across the warm white sand to the sea and paddled and splashed in it to cool off and refresh from our travels. We took our showers then walked further down the beach to a restaurant. Here they displayed an assortment of fish that had been caught that day and you could pick the one you wanted then they went and cooked it for you. We sat down at a table with a view over the sea and ordered Kingfisher beers.

After spending five months in arid surroundings with no fish or meat and no beer, this was indeed a treat. I chose a snapper fish and it was delicious. They brought a 1 litre bottle of local beer, which we shared delightedly. As we were finishing this, a woman walked by with a huge bowl of fruit on her head. She lowered it down for us to see and we chose some fresh pineapple and bananas, which had obviously just been picked, they were so fresh and tasty. We made a habit of eating there most nights as it was so reasonable, delicious and had an unbeatable setting.

Having satisfied our thirst and hunger, we slowly wandered back to our hotel and settled in for the night. We had the most restful night as you could hear the sea gently lapping on the shore through the open –netted window. In the morning we ordered our hot water and had showers then the landlady provided us with chai and a simple breakfast of rice-based cereal.

In Jalahalli, we had to dress very modestly, with shorts and tank tops being strictly forbidden. We weren't sure what was acceptable here so we put on our swim-suits and covered them up with a wrap-around skirt and loose cotton shirt. We took a small bag with us for towels, books, water and some cash and headed down to the main part of the beach. There were little stalls there where you could buy refreshments, trinkets and clothing.

We spread out our towels and lay down on the sand and watched life all around us. There was a fishing boat just off-shore and about ten men were pulling in the net with long ropes. It looked like a tug-of-war. It took a while for them to pull the catch right up on to the beach and the net was teeming with fish of all different types. They untangled the fish and threw them into large metal bowls, which the women then put on their heads and carried up into the town to sell. The men then had to sort the net out and fold it up and put it back in the boat and pulled away from shore again, whether to do more fishing or to go home, we don't know.

A few people were in the sea but the women were still wearing their saris and the men wore shorts. There weren't so many people on the beach so we decided to move away from the main activity and kept our clothes on until we got close to the water then dropped our skirts, shirts and towels in a pile nearby and plunged in. It was like submerging in a warm bath and felt wonderful. We thought as long as we stayed under water, we wouldn't bother anyone so we swam and swam until we got tired then swam into shore as close as we could before standing up and quickly wrapped ourselves around with towels then donned our wrap-around skirts and shirts before walking back up the beach. The sun soon dried us and we daringly pulled our skirts up to our knees and opened up our shirts but didn't dare do more than that in case we offended the locals.

After lying in the sun, we wandered up to the stalls to look around. The first thing I bought was a large sun-hat. They also had brightly coloured sarongs and cotton dresses so I bought one of each. There was also a stall selling cold drinks and snacks, including locally grown cashews, so we enjoyed a cool lime soda, without ice, some vegetable pakora, followed by slices of pineapple, a banana each and a bag of cashews to nibble on later. We wandered around a bit then sat back down on the beach to watch more life pass by. It didn't take long then for the merchants to find us with their trays of carved animals, shell jewellery, silver and more food items. It took a while to convince them that we didn't need any more. After this it became a daily occurrence for them to pester us on the beach, which was annoying but understandable – they have to make a living somehow.

When it got too hot, we walked back to our room and lay down and read and slept for a while. The sea breeze through the window cooled off the room nicely. The room was all tiled so it didn't absorb any heat from the sun and there were awnings over the windows providing adequate shade. The roof was also shaded by the surrounding palm trees.

I was looking forward to the evening walk back to our previous night's restaurant and the anticipation of the rare treats of fresh fish, fruit and cool beer. It didn't disappoint. It was going to be difficult to leave this piece of heaven away from the crowds and set in these idyllic surroundings. However, after a few more days of exploring, relaxing, eating and paddling, it was time to bid farewell to our friendly host and to find our way back across the rice paddy to the village.

Kovalom, at this time, was still unspoilt and just had one luxury hotel up on the cliff but now the secret is out and it has become a popular tourist destination. I haven't been back there since 1994 but I don't think I want to either as I prefer to keep these memories of a special paradise, made all the more exquisite by the culinary depravations of the previous six months.

We caught the bus from Kovalom back to Trivandrum and were immediately immersed back into the hustle and bustle of a busy city and train station. This time we took the night train straight back to Bangalore, spent a night there and then took the overnight train back up to Raichur and the bus from Rachur to Jalahalli. It was just a short walk from the village of Jalahalli across the field to campus and we didn't have too much luggage so we arrived back unannounced and just in time for breakfast. There was much chatter at the Mess as everyone wanted to hear all about our trip and live vicariously through our adventures. We enjoyed reliving it by the telling but missed the fresh fruit. We had however brought back a large amount of cashews for everyone to share.

9
CAMPUS LIFE:

"Give the ones you love wings to fly, roots to come back and reasons to stay" HH Dalai Lama

Every month Samuha held Sector Head meetings for the leaders of all the different programs. Sometimes these meetings were held over two days. We sat on the floor in a large circle, except for Mahesh who needed a chair to sit on. Everyone seemed to be able to sit cross-legged on the floor for hours. Every two hours Venkoba came round with trays of chai or occasionally salt or sweet lime drinks. Lunch & dinner were served outside on leaf plates, sewn together with sticks, and it was good to stretch ones legs and move around. Sometimes these meetings went on until midnight – and then started again at 8am.

All decisions were made by consensus and arguments about the use of certain words could easily last up to an hour. Pradeep chaired the meetings, which were run in English but sometimes translations had to be done for those who had limited understanding of English. Fortunately Pradeep had great faith in Narayanswamy and the Disability Sector so there was never any interference in our program but quite often the Health program would have to change tactics on a monthly basis, which was very frustrating for the English Doctors and nurse who worked in Health.

Samuha's disability program often ran camps for children, where families brought their children with disability to stay for the week-end and we provided assessments, therapy and support groups for the families. When we were preparing for the first one, I felt we should also provide some play and recreation activities for the children so I asked Ayyalappa to make a couple of swing sets. He did this by suspending ropes from the beams of the roof over the patio of the clinic and made swings out of tyres, which the child could safely sit in. I got this idea out of David Werner's book, Disabled Village Children, which was my main reference book for many ideas for aids and appliances for the program.

There was also a concrete tank on campus full of fish. The idea was to raise fish to sell but nobody seemed to be doing much about this project so I suggested that we should drain and clean the tank then put fresh water in it so that children could use it for hydrotherapy. Everyone seemed to think this was a good idea so before we went to the village that morning Narayanswamy asked Venkoba to drain and clean the tank and refill it with clean water.

After our day's work we came back to campus and were amazed to see that sure enough the tank had been cleaned and was full of clean water but they had also put the fish back in it! Narayanswamy didn't seem to think that this was a big deal and said that the children could still use it and play amongst the fish! I wasn't going to argue with him so that is what we did. The children came the following morning and enjoyed playing in the sun-warmed water and didn't seem fazed by the fish. We did some water assisted range of motion exercises with them. You could fit two small children in the tank at a time. The swings were also a great hit!

Another mis-communication happened prior to another camp. We needed a western toilet to enable people with disability to sit rather than squat Asian style, as people with paralysed legs couldn't squat. Mahesh had a contraption for his toilet which was a seat with a hole in it, which he could place over the toilet but others could still remove it and squat if they so wished. We wanted to keep his toilet facility just for Samuha staff so we needed to build another one for visitors with disability. Samuha bought a Western toilet and instructed the labourers to build a shed and dig a hole in the ground where the toilet could sit and provide drainage from it to the cess pit outside the compound. Again we left for the day to do our village visits and when we came back at the end of the day, Venkoba proudly took Narayanswamy to see their days work. They had never installed a western toilet before so they had dug a deep hole and buried the toilet right up to the rim – so you would still need to squat over it to use it! We had good laughs about that, that evening sitting around Mahesh's hut.

At one of these social gatherings in Mahesh's hut, he told us that he was getting married. There was much excitement and Mahesh was beaming. His wife to be, Prema, would come to campus and live with him there but his house needed to be modified to make it larger, with a kitchen to accommodate the two of them. Mahesh took leave for marriage preparations and all that that entails.

While he was gone the construction workers got busy and dug up around the foundations of his hut so they could expand the walls. One night, after I was already in bed, Margaret and Henrietta, the two English Doctors who now shared my room, came in and started screaming. There was an army of ants crawling through our door, across the floor and up the concrete wall of Henrietta's bed and then under her mattress towards the kitchen. There were millions of them streaming from Mahesh's hut across the path to our hut, about a foot wide army of them and two inches thick as they crawled on top of each other. The two doctors grabbed their night attire and fled. I was so tired, I didn't want to get up and anyway the army wasn't diverging from its path. When I got up in the morning they were all gone without a trace and the doctors returned from their shared space in the girls' dorm at the other end of the campus.

Narayanswamy was also at the marrying age. He had resisted pressure from his family for an arranged marriage but now two of his colleagues were actively searching for a suitable wife for him, as is the Indian custom. There were several single girls living on campus, working as social workers, but it is not the Indian custom for men to socialise with girls except on purely business terms. For all social events the women sit on one side and the men on the other. Even for eating at the Mess, segregation was the norm.

I sent weekly reports to Action Health on the development of the program and part way through my stay, Paul, one of the Action Health staff, came from England to check up on the progress. Action Health and Samuha had an excellent working relationship and Samuha was held up as being one of their main success stories.

One of the highlights of each week was the cultural evenings every Saturday night. On this night we all ate at the same time and sat on rugs outside the Mess in a large rectangle. Mudurangappa signalled the call to dinner by banging on a drum and shouting out a Hindu prayer at the top of his lungs. We ate off the traditional leaf plates. The food was ladled out of huge pots on to these plates and we were given a special treat of a curried boiled egg each. After eating, the plates were just folded up and thrown in the bin as they were totally bio-degradable. After dinner was the cultural program. They all loved to sing and had beautiful voices. They expected us to join in but none of us were musical and it was always an embarrassment. One fellow played the tabla drums and another played the harmonium. Many of the songs were led by one singer then everyone joined in the choruses. They must have all been popular folk songs as everyone seemed to know them well.

Leading up to the cultural program, us westerners always fretted as to what we could do because they always wanted us to participate. One time I co-erced Somanna, the assistant cook, to have a conversation with me as entertainment for the program. He wasn't allowed to speak Kannada and I wasn't allowed to speak English. We managed to keep it up for over five minutes amongst hoots of laughter.

Another time I decided to write a poem. Narayanswamy was planning to leave the campus for a while and I wrote a poem about his imminent departure:

WE WILL WELCOME YOU HOME

We will welcome you back to your abode
When you've come to the end of your travelling mode.

Your friends will welcome you with open arms
Their worries will vanish with your charms
Soon they'll hear the familiar laughter
And everyone will be smiling after.

Tales and adventures you will be sharing
Lifestyles and customs be comparing.
Your morning will start with the familiar chai
Just as the sun brightens the sky.

We can see you sitting sleepy-eyed,
Wrapped in your shawl as your thoughts confide.
It'll take weeks of story-telling
Which all of campus will find compelling.

With pleasure you'll use your native tongue
Glad with your friends to be among.
They'll be so happy to have you back
You will help them keep on the right track.

It'll take a while to settle down
But the experiences will add to your crown
You will have grown and changed maybe
But still the loved and respected Narayanswamy.

Of course, once it was translated into Kannada, it didn't rhyme anymore. I hadn't thought about that but Narayanswamy liked it. It's thanks to those cultural evenings that I started writing as it was always such a struggle to think of something appropriate to do and once I started writing poems, I enjoyed it and carried on.

Narayanswamy wanted to take a course in England on Overseas Development and then go to Uganda to work for a few months. I thought this was a great idea and encouraged him and offered to help him financially. These plans were still in their infancy but were percolating.

10
REVERSE CULTURE SHOCK:

"The best way to find yourself is to lose yourself in the service of others" Mahatma Gandhi

My six month contract with Action Health was beginning to draw to a close. I didn't feel ready to leave and Action Health hadn't yet found a replacement for me. Narayanswamy wanted to take a leave of absence and he asked me if I would be willing to stay on and take charge of the program.

I was in a quandary. I really wanted to stay but had no idea what Floyd would think about that. It was nearly Christmastime and I wanted to go home. I could always just go home for a month and then return to India for another six months. It was so difficult without phone service and e-mail hadn't yet been invented. Narayanswamy drove me by jeep to Raichur. I needed to find out how Floyd was managing and whether he regretted or enjoyed my absence. I went to the pay phone kiosk and called my home number. The phone rang and rang then I heard my own voice on the other end asking me to leave a message. What to do? I couldn't keep driving back to Raichur on a daily basis to try and connect.

I told the machine, "I have been asked to stay another six months with Samuha. I have to decide so they can make appropriate plans. I don't know what to do but I think I will come home for Christmas for a month then return here for another six months. I wish you were home so I could talk to you."

The next few days were probably the worst of my time in India while I worried about what decision to make. I tried to weigh up the pros and cons of staying. I wanted to stay – I loved it here - but what about Floyd and his feelings? If I stayed, Narayanswamy could take a sabbatical to pursue his studies in UK and work in Uganda. I thought it would be a wonderful opportunity for him. In the end I told Narayanswamy that I would go home for a month but then come back for six months so he could take his sabbatical and I would run the program. I made my decision and booked my return flight home to Canada for Christmas. I would return to Samuha in January.

I told Action Health about this decision, which they were happy to hear. They asked me when I came back to India, if I would evaluate a program in Kerala for them as this organisation had applied to Action Health for assistance in training and developing their new community based rehabilitation program. I agreed to do this. This gave me another purpose to return to India.

In late November, I took the train to Bangalore to attend a Samuha Board meeting and to do some shopping and book my flight home. I spent a couple of nights there and got everything organised but when the auto-rickshaw dropped me off at the station to take the train back to Raichur, my purse slipped off my shoulder on to the seat as I struggled with my luggage. I noticed I didn't have it as I crossed the parking lot but when I looked back there were scores of identical black and yellow autos pulling in and out of various lines. I had no idea, which was mine and it had probably already left anyway. What a sinking feeling.

I went to the station manager and told him what had happened. My train ticket and money were in my purse as well as my passport, my return air ticket home and some travellers cheques. It was already 10pm and my train was about to pull out of the station. The station manager suggested I sleep in the Ladies waiting room on the platform for the night and that is what I did. I lay down on the concrete floor clutching my luggage and worried about all the eventualities. When I woke in the morning, I realised I had enough change in my pocket to phone the Samuha office in Bangalore, which I did.

Geetha answered the phone and told me to stay where I was and not to worry. Someone from Samuha would come and help me. In about half an hour Samson, the administrator, found me and told me he would dedicate his day to helping me. The first thing we did was to go to the police station to report the loss. Of course he asked me for identifying features of the auto. I started to explain then quickly realised they were all identical. We then went to Thomas Cook and cancelled the travellers cheques and got some new ones. Then to the Airlines office and fortunately they re-issued my tickets without much hassle. The only thing left now was my passport. This was more difficult as the passport office was in Delhi, a four hour flight away or a three day train journey.

Samson took me back to the hotel as I would have to spend another night there and get the train back to Raichur the following night. After Samson dropped me off, I walked down the street to where I caught the auto from originally. There was a huge garbage pile, I searched through to see if it might contain my purse. Of course it didn't.

I was feeling pretty dejected and worried but there was nothing more to be done than to return to Jalahalli and plan how I would get to Delhi in time to renew my passport before flying home to Canada. I took the overnight train to Raichur then the bus from there to Jalahalli. Narayanswamy said he had to go to Delhi the following week for meetings and that he had always wanted to visit Agra and the Taj Mahal. He arranged for a flight from Bangalore to Delhi the following week. This still gave me a few days before my flight home.

It looked as though everything was going to work out. I wrapped up my work and made plans with the team for the weeks I would be away. I said "goodbye" to everyone in Jalahalli and told them I would be back in a month. I packed up all my stuff and took the train back down to Bangalore and then flew on to Delhi. I met Narayanswamy there and together we went to the consulate office. To begin with they said they couldn't help me and I would have to come back tomorrow. Tomorrow was a problem because we wanted to go to Agra to see the Taj Mahal, as I had to fly out the next day. It was beginning to look as though this combination of events was going to be impossible until I offered my registration form. This is a form that is given to you if you register at the local police station within a few days of your arrival in India. It is compulsory if you stay longer than six months but otherwise it's optional. This seemed to make all the difference. The officer's eyes lit up and within a few minutes I had a newly issued passport – what a relief.

Finally I could relax. We had a celebratory beer over dinner and planned an early departure in the morning for Agra. We caught the bus at 6 am for the 200 km journey. The journey took about five hours through congested traffic but the sight of the Taj was well worth it. It is a classic white marble building built as a tomb for the Shah's wife. It is intricately carved and exquisitely beautiful with a large central dome and four tall domed pillars at each corner of the surrounding parapet. A moat runs up the entrance to the Taj allowing reflections of the white marble in its waters. Manicured gardens run alongside the moat and convenient paths allow good access and photographic opportunities.

Another famous site at Agra is the Fort, which we also visited but the Taj is where you want to spend your time. After a few hours, it was time to leave again and we took the bus back to Delhi arriving well after dark. The trip was a great gift after the stress of the passport saga.

The following morning I took a taxi to the International airport and started my journey back to Canada via Dubai then Vancouver. Floyd drove down to Vancouver and met me at the airport. We hugged each other tight. We stayed in a hotel overnight but we were shy and trod carefully as we gradually got used to each other again. We were both happy to see each other but we both harboured our own thoughts.

We started the long drive north to Summit Lake, about a twelve hour journey. This was now December so the temperature change after the heat from India was a shock. It struck me that the sidewalks looked empty with no colourful people wandering by and it was strange to see only vehicles and no animals being herded down the road.

The further north we went, the whiter the landscape became and by the time we reached Summit Lake the snow banks were at least a metre deep. We stopped on the way in Prince George, our nearest town, for a few groceries and I felt as though I was among giants as I walked down the aisles. Everyone here was so much bigger than people in India. It was good to eventually get back to our log house on the lake and to stoke up the wood stove and feel the comforting warmth of the fire.

This was a couple of weeks before Christmas and I soon realised that the small gifts I had thoughtfully bought in Bangalore for all the family were not going to be sufficient as people's expectations were so much greater here. I was going to have to go on a shopping spree. The plan was to go to Rocky Mountain House for Christmas, where half of the family lived. This involved a spectacular drive through the Rockies, which made me realise how lucky I was to live here so close to the snow-clad mountains. It was wonderful to see everyone again and we had a happy time together. I started to wonder if I had made the right decision to go back to India for another six months but I had made the commitment and there was no turning back.

When I hadn't been able to reach Floyd on the phone from Raichur and had to make the decision without discussing it with him, he later told me that he wasn't too happy with my decision but there we are. We did a little x-country ski-ing and visited friends but before long it was time to pack up again and plan the return trip to India. This time I would fly to Bombay then take a domestic flight to Calicut on the Kerala coast to evaluate the organisation there, as I had previously promised to Action Health. After a few days there, I would fly on to Bangalore.

In mid-January Floyd took me to the airport in Prince George and I made my connections from there. I knew I was taking a risk with our relationship but Floyd is a gregarious soul and had many good friends and interests. I think he enjoyed his freedom too. This was going to be another six months but this time I knew the score in India. Although I was worried about leaving Floyd, I also looked forward to seeing my friends at Samuha.

11
RETURN TO INDIA:

"Let me assert my firm belief that the only thing we have to fear is fear itself" FD Roosevelt

I had to be up at 4.30am in order to catch the flight from Prince George to Vancouver. After several hours wait in Vancouver, I boarded the plane and settled down for the long flight to Heathrow. I had a few hours there before catching the next flight to Dubai. I was amazed at the grandeur of Dubai airport, I then boarded an early morning flight from there to Bombay. On arrival in Bombay, I took a taxi across the city to the domestic airport and waited a few hours for the two hour flight to Calicut, on the West coast of Kerala. There I was met by Mr Aseez, the manager of the program, which I was there to evaluate. He took me straight to my hotel. I was in bed by 6pm totally exhausted from the long journey, two full days of flying and waiting in airports. I slept through until 6am.

Mr Aseez picked me up at 9am and took me to see various aspects of the project in Calicut. It was a huge project with several vocational training programs. They also ran a coconut plantation so we enjoyed a sweet long drink of coconut juice and walked out on to the beach. I was introduced to Dr Kutty who showed me the community based rehabilitation program and the three of us later went out for dinner. I stayed there two days while they showed me all aspects of their program. It was most interesting and set in beautiful surroundings.

I started on my report for Action Health before boarding my flight to Bangalore the following morning. That night I took the train to Raichur and was met there by Pasha, the jeep driver, at 5am. It was an enjoyable familiar drive to Jallahalli and we arrived there at 7am to a great welcome with "welcome home" signs in my room. It was lovely to be back. I distributed the gifts I had brought with me from Canada, mostly shirts and key rings. The next day all the janitorial staff were proudly wearing my shirts. I thought I'd brought gifts for their kids but the T-shirts fitted the men perfectly – they are all so slender!

I completed my Calicut report and sent it on to Action Health. I soon fell into the usual routine and enjoyed my daily trips to the villages on the motor-bike to see families in their homes as well as teaching the regular training programs. That week-end there was a big Hindu festival and a group of us went out to Tintini, a Temple on the Krishna River. We crossed the river on a coracle boat, which is a round boat made from bamboo and covered with tar-impregnated canvas. It is steered with a single wooden pole and the passengers squat around the inside edge of the boat. Feet and legs always get wet but this is part of the fun. People take their motorbikes across the river on these boats and sometimes even their animals.

Another place we frequently went to on field trips for special occasions was Hampi. This is an important archaeological site, situated close to the project in South India. In the 12th century this was a flourishing kingdom, which ruled the southern part of India, reaching its peak in the early 16th century. It was then ransacked by Muslim invaders and many of the buildings were destroyed at that time. The present site covers about twelve square kilometers and includes many temples depicting elephants, deities and intricate scenes from Indian mythology. There are also elaborate palaces, large royal baths and massive elephant stables. UNESCO has recognized this site as being of important historical and archaeological interest. The Indian government is in the process of restoring some of the buildings to their former glory.

The whole area is surrounded by rice paddy, banana plantations and fields of bright yellow sunflowers. It is situated on the banks of the broad Tungabhadra River, which can be crossed by coracle boat to reach two smaller villages on the opposite bank. These villages are also of historical interest and offer an assortment of charming lodges and restaurants for the visitor. I always head for a unique restaurant situated on the bank of the river where you can observe river life while eating excellent food off a banana leaf plate while sitting on the ground with a table straddled over your legs.

We always see a variety of bird life as well as herds of wandering goats. We can watch the buffalo being washed in the river while people wash their clothes along the river bank and the coracle boats peacefully ply their way across. Walking this vast site offers magnificent views of the whole valley with many temples perched on the rocky hills. Trails criss-cross the area and one can leisurely enjoy the scenery as well as appreciate the history and exceptional architecture. The buildings are adorned with elaborate and exquisite stone carvings.

Hampi used to be rich with gold, silver, precious jewels and pearls. Double rows of stone pillars remain depicting the market where these jewels were traded. Now the main bazaar stretches along both sides of the royal road. Here one can buy woven blankets, cotton clothing, hand-made paper, jewellery and bags of every description. These shops are intermingled with money-changers, internet cafes and international phones, to cater to the many tourists. It is strange after several weeks of village life, wearing modest Indian clothing, to suddenly encounter tourists. Some of whom show bare flesh, have red sunburned faces and are well-fed instead of the usual graceful, yet undernourished village populace.

A day in Hampi provides a pleasant interlude from our otherwise busy schedule of providing therapy inputs for people with disability. I hadn't really noticed the beauty and variety of birds in India previously. Kingfishers are surprising as this is a drought prone area and often there are no rains so the small rivers and ponds are dry. However there is an abundance of kingfishers. The smaller ones are a vivid glossy green with white throat. The larger ones are blue with white breast and there are also the pied variety with striking black and white markings. They are often seen perched on the overhead wires and must be feeding on frogs and grass-hoppers as there are certainly no fish.

Bright green parakeets are also frequently seen in small flocks. The hoopoe is an unusual looking bird with black & white markings including its crowning spiked crest. White egrets accompany the cattle often riding on their backs or walking around between them, eating grubs and insects disturbed by the cattle. We have also seen some unusual pheasants with dark brown wings and plum red head. A few quail were observed on the edge of the road and there are also numerous pigeons and doves.

There are a variety of birds that I haven't been able to identify such as some glossy green birds with a long forked tail frequently perched on the overhead wires. There is also a beautiful blue bird that was mostly observed on the ground. When the wings are folded they are dark blue but in flight they exhibit vivid bright blue strips with some white bars. It is about the size of a blue jay and very striking.

There is no shortage of insects for the birds to feed on. Mosquitoes are a problem as they not only carry malaria but several other diseases such as dengue, Japanese encephalitis, elephantitis and another disease called Chikkengunya which has been endemic and causes severe joint pain and stiffness. There are even green mosquitoes that live in the trees but bite just as viciously as their cousins. Most villagers sleep on a mat on the floor. Huts are not equipped with windows, just openings, so mosquitoes have free range. Villagers cannot afford repellent or nets so clothing and a bed sheet are their only protection. Mosquitoes spread disease by biting an infected person and then biting others, injecting the parasite, in the case of malaria and elephantitis or the virus, in the case of Dengue and Chikkengunya. Sometimes other animals are involved as the host such as pigs for Japanese encephalitis and monkeys for Chikkengunya.

The most common serious diseases are malaria and typhoid. Malnutrition is also common as well as respiratory and gastro-intestinal infections. Contaminated water from open wells used to be the main source of disease such as typhoid and polio but now bore-wells have been drilled in most of the villages to provide a clean source of water. The only problem with these bore-wells is that sometimes the water table is so low that minerals such as fluoride and, less frequently, arsenic can contaminate the water. Fluorosis and arsenicosis are now common in some villages. Later on, Pradeep sent Chandamma and I on a mission to study the fluorosis in a particularly contaminated area.

12
FURTHER EXPANSION AND FLUOROSIS:

"I have often wondered whether a person is justified in neglecting his own family to fight for opportunities for others" Nelson Mandela

Gradually we took on more staff including two new orthotic trainees who participated in all the training sessions. We also added two senior disability workers, Pranesh and Chandrashekar, who had their Masters of Social Work degrees so they were able to take on more responsible positions. One day Narayanswamy & I went with Pradeep to Raichur to find a suitable location to build another workshop. Our work revolved around a 60 km radius of each workshop so building this second workshop had the ability to increase our reach considerably.

Gradually Narayanswamy made his plans for visiting England to take an Overseas Development course before moving on to Uganda to work in a Development Organisation there. Pradeep and Narayanswamy were putting lots of pressure on me to stay on as Sector Head of the disability program, while Narayanswamy was away. I was certainly torn between staying on and returning home. My visa was valid until mid-April so I extended it for another few months to give me a chance to decide my future. I loved being with Samuha, they were just like family and the work was so needed but I still had a life waiting for me back home and that's where I belonged.

I had suggested to Action Health that Samuha needed an Occupational Therapy trainer next so in April I was pleased to hear that Juliette would be coming for six months to be the trainer. In the meantime Narayanswamy & I made several visits to the Spastics Society in Bangalore, to a Speech and Hearing Centre in Hyderabad and a Mental Health organization in Mysore. This was to facilitate resource people to come to Jalahalli to train the team and also for selected team members to spend time with each organization, according to their needs, to strengthen the team. These connections became very useful for building the capacity of the community based rehabilitation program.

I attended a couple of the Samuha Board meetings in Bangalore. These were long but interesting meetings. While in Bangalore, I also visited the Association for the Physically Handicapped, APH, which was founded by Hema. She herself was disabled by polio and needed a wheel-chair for mobility. She was an amazing woman and ran this excellent facility, which had a school for disabled children, a slum program, an orthotic workshop and vocational training program. APH and Samuha worked very closely together over the years and Hema and Pradeep were on each other's Boards but both being very strong personalities, they sometimes got into some hot disagreements!

It wasn't all work either. Narayanswamy, Mahesh and I with others travelled by train to Phani's wedding and also to Elango's marriage. Mangala, one of the girls in the health program, invited the English doctors and I to her wedding in Mangalore on the West coast. It took several long bus rides to get there and the wedding ceremonies lasted several days but it was all very interesting. They dressed us up in saris for the main occasion, which are very elegant and anything less is not considered suitable attire for a wedding ceremony. They took us to see a Temple out in the ocean and we also visited Jog Falls, which is a beautiful nature area in the forest in the Western Ghats. After the ceremonies were completed we returned to campus by bus.

It finally became time for Narayanswamy to leave in mid-April. Elan gave a farewell party for him at his house. We saw him off on the train at Raichur station and then it was up to me to run the disability program. The following day there was a big festival in Jalahalli, involving water fights and two lines of men pulling on thick ropes to move a huge stone chariot across the field. This is an annual event and I was allowed to participate in the pulling of the chariot briefly, but you wouldn't want to slip and get crushed. It was warming up lots now and that night I slept outside in the moonlight, much cooler and beautiful.

A week after Narayanswamy left, Juliette, the Occupational Therapist, arrived. I met her at the airport in Bangalore and we spent a few days there to help her acclimatize. Pradeep had recently moved from Jalahalli to Bangalore and he invited us to his home for dinner. Phani, Elango and Mahesh were also there so it was a great introduction for Juliette. The next day we did some shopping for suitable clothes and other needs. We also visited Samraksha, Samuha's HIV/AIDS project which offers respite care and education for the clients.

After this we took the overnight train up to Raichur and were met there by Pasha and the jeep, which took us back to Jalahalli. It was extremely hot now. We did an assessment clinic together and on the Saturday I did my last training program as that would then become Juliette's purview. After a brief orientation, Juliette became the trainer and I did more administrative work such as staff evaluations and writing reports. We both did village visits but went with different disability workers to see different clients. Juliette also loved being there and taught the team their much needed basic occupational therapy skills. Also during this time, we started a tailoring centre for vocational training for older girls with disability. At the end of their six month program, they were given a sewing machine to use in their village so they could then support themselves financially.

The rains started in early May, it was such a relief. It started with a thunderstorm then torrential rain for a couple of hours. Everyone came outside and revelled in it! Towards the end of May we went on another field trip for the day, this time to Badami. This is a special area where beautiful Temples are carved into the rocks. It is like a series of rock shelters with exquisite carvings and pillars. The rock ceilings are high and each Temple is spacious and ornate. They are situated on the banks of the Krishna River. The only problem is the aggressive monkeys. We saw one large monkey take a purse from a lady then it bounded on top of the rocks, where no-one could reach it. The thief undid the wallet and took out paper rupee notes one by one and scattered them on the rocks where the wind lifted them up and blew them away. I doubt it was the first time this had happened!

The next day, we left Juliette in charge and Chandamma and I left by jeep for Bellary, where Pradeep had asked us to perform a study regarding fluorosis, which was prevalent in this area. Fluorosis is caused by too high content of fluoride in the water. Over time, this starts with joint pain and stiffness but can continue to cause calcification of the ligaments of the spine and hips with gradual loss of movement and increasing flexion of the trunk. This condition can even progress to causing paralysis of the legs due to increased pressure on the spinal cord. Fluorosis is entirely preventable but cannot be treated. We stayed at the Cluny Convent in Bellary and visited the Bengali camps. We met with pertinent government officials, concerned with health and sanitation. They were very co-operative and fed us useful information. We also met some clients with fluorosis who exhibited premature ageing and a stooped posture. Fluorosis in children causes pitting of the teeth, which can be an early sign of this condition.

The acceptable level of fluoride in the water in India is 1.5 parts per million, ppm. Areas with 3.5 ppm or more are found to have many cases of crippling arthritis attributable to fluoride. In the USA and probably in Canada too, they add 1 ppm fluoride to the water supply and up to 4 ppm is considered acceptable. The difference may be that due to the heat and poverty, Indians consume far more water than North Americans as that is all they drink, either as tea or plain water. In some of the villages we visited, the fluoride content was found to be as high as 10 ppm.

The Indian and State government were aware of the problem and were doing research into effective filtration systems to remove the fluoride from the water. We were able to take documented results of these surveys back to Pradeep as part of our report. The fluoride needed to be filtered out at the source, because families couldn't afford individual filtration systems. One of the problems that hadn't been tackled yet was what to do with the excess fluoride, as you didn't want that to seep back into the water table. This problem had still not been solved so more villagers were experiencing the symptoms of fluorosis.

After gathering all the information we could, we returned to Jalahalli and wrote up our detailed report for Pradeep, with suggestions for future remedial action. Our next task was to host a couple of Speech and Hearing experts who were coming from Calcutta the next day to meet and evaluate some of the children and to teach their skills to the disability workers. Our days were always full and varied.

I decided that I would return to Canada in June so I needed to re-book my airline tickets and make the needed preparations. Pradeep wanted me to try and set up charities in England and Canada to support Samuha's work so I had to allow time for this too. I also needed time to debrief with Action Health in UK. I was noticing that I was getting more tired daily and I had lost considerable weight so I felt, for my health, that I needed to return home. I hadn't been seriously sick at all but I was getting increasingly bored with the plain white rice and had lost interest in the food.

13
BABUMIYA:

"Strength does not come from physical capacity, it comes from an indomitable will" Mahatma Gandhi

At the end of May, on my birthday, the English doctors and I were enjoying a rare special meal outside our hut. Habeeb Pasha, Babumiya's brother, came running breathlessly, "Madam, Madam come quickly. Babumiya has been injured by a bull." That is how it was translated to us as we sat on the patio eating a special treat of curried chicken on this vegetarian campus. The two English doctors, Henrietta and Margaret, had managed to bake a cake in a solar oven for me as I was celebrating my 50th birthday away from home. There was no phone service so the only way to communicate with Babumiya's family was to drive to the village.

We took a last bite of delicious rare cake then jumped up and collected some dressings and first aid equipment and climbed into the jeep and set off to Babumiya's village. We wended our way through herds of sheep and goats, avoiding bullock carts and farm workers returning home from their fields. Babumiya was one of the trainee disability workers with the community based rehabilitation program working with children with polio in rural villages in the arid Deccan Plateau. It was a bumpy dusty drive. As we arrived at his village, half an hour later, we saw a cluster of people huddled around Babumiya who was lying on the ground. I presumed that he had been gored but there was no blood anywhere. It soon became apparent that he had been thrown by this bull. He had been tossed in the air and landed awkwardly

"O Madam, thank you for coming."
"What happened Babumiya. Did you get attacked by a bull?"
"Yes Madam. It threw me up and on to the ground."
'Do you have pain anywhere?"
"No, I can't feel anything."
"If we help you, can you roll on to your back?"
"I wouldn't let anyone touch me but you know what to do Madam. My family will help. Just tell them what you need."

Henrietta, the English Doctor, helped me and we asked three more of Babu's relatives to assist. I took care of the head with Henrietta at the feet and one villager at the shoulders and one at the hips. I explained how we needed to roll Babumiya like a log. First of all we slowly straightened him out then rolled him in unison on to his back. On examination, Babumiya couldn't feel or move his legs and he had very limited feeling or movement in his arms. It quickly became obvious that he had broken his neck. We were in a remote village with no medical equipment or expertise in the area.

"Babumiya we need a board to place underneath you and bags of sand to immobilize your spine." He relayed this to his brother in Kannada. In no time, someone had found a door we could use and several of the men filled up bags with sand. Again we log-rolled Babu on to his side, making sure that no movement took place in his spine, especially his neck. Two of the men then placed the door under Babu's back and we log-rolled him back on to it. We secured sand-bags on either side of his head, down either side of his trunk and hips. We then secured some cloth round his forehead and under the sand-bags so his head couldn't move.

"Babumiya, you are safe now and your back and neck are secured. We'll lift you into the back of the jeep and drive back to campus. There we will decide what the next steps should be."
"Thank you Madam. My wife will come with me."

The men picked up the door with Babu safely secured on it and we ensured that his head couldn't move. They then slid the door into the back of the jeep. Babu's wife and brother climbed up into the jeep beside him to ensure that he was safe and feeling secure. The jeep then slowly drove the tortuous journey back to Samuha campus

As we travelled down the road, we heard the full story. Babumiya was leading the bull with a rope from its shed to water when this happened. Suddenly the bull charged towards Babumiya and knocked him down. He managed to sit back up but then the bull came again, picked him up by the horns and threw him. Again he was able to sit back up but then the bull came a third time and pushed Babumiya's head down to his knees. The family had seen this happen and came running.

Babumiya cried out and wouldn't let any of the villagers move him. He could speak but couldn't feel his legs and was scared that he had damaged his spine. The villagers kept trying to lift him up but Babumiya pleaded with them not to move him. His brother showed up about fifteen minutes after the accident and Babumiya asked him to go to Samuha and get help. He did that but it's a half hour drive away so by the time I arrived on the scene, nearly two hours had already passed.

Once we got to campus, Pradeep, the head of Samuha, arranged to transport him to Raichur, the nearest town with a railway station. This necessitated a further two hour jeep ride but at least this was on paved road but still rough. He was then precariously lifted, still on the door, up on to the coach and down the narrow corridor to a berth on the overnight train to Bangalore. Fortunately they had room for him in the First Class compartment on the MP allocation so still on the door, he could lie on the bottom bunk. Trains always run full so it was lucky that this berth was available for him. The train journey takes ten hours, with many stops, arriving in Bangalore at 6am. He was met there by Samuha staff who transferred him to the ambulance, still on the door, which took him to the Neurological Hospital, sixteen hours after his injury.

The next night I took the train to Bangalore and went to the Ramaiah Hospital to visit Babumiya and spoke with the Doctor. The surgeon decided that surgery wasn't necessary so his neck was immobilized with traction. This necessitated a halo type contraption screwed through his skull with weights applied to immobilize his neck. I stayed in Bangalore three days and visited Babumiya each day. He wasn't doing well and was feeling depressed. He also developed a cough. I stayed at Pradeep's while I was there then needed to take the train back to Raichur and bus to Jalahalli to continue the work at Samuha.

We ran some more children's assessment clinics and attended another Sector head meeting and a couple more days of work and reports then I took the train back down to Bangalore and visited Babumiya again. This time he was feeling much better. The Doctor explained that the traction would remain for several weeks then after six weeks he could be discharged back to Samuha with his neck in a rigid collar. I visited with Babumiya for a couple more days then took the bus from Bangalore back to Jalahalli. I hated to leave Babumiya but he was in good hands.

14
END OF FOURTEEN MONTHS WITH SAMUHA IN INDIA:

Mr Gandhi what do you think of western civilization? "I think it would be a good idea" Mahatma Gandhi

After leaving Babumiya, I returned to Jalahalli to wrap up loose ends and pass the work on to Juliette. I also signed a contract with Chandrashekar so that he would be senior disability worker and act as Sector Head until Narayanswamy returned from his travels. The CBR team gave an elaborate leaving party for me with lots of singing and a chicken dinner. We exchanged gifts and sadly said our "good-byes." This was now June so the heat was gradually abating but there were still a couple more weeks of probable rain.

Ashok and Chandamma came with me to Raichur in the jeep and saw me off on the train to Bombay, an 18 hour journey. The train left at 9pm so we had supper before I left then pushed our way through the hectic throngs to my train and I climbed aboard. After securing my luggage under the seat with a chain and padlock, I climbed on to the top berth and settled down for the night. I was glad I had the top berth as then I could lie down whenever I wanted to and was less likely to get bothered by merchants selling their wares.

The chai wallahs started coming by early in the morning and by 8am I was ready for a coffee and a surprisingly good omelette they prepared on the station. I had a good book to read on Gandhi and there were always interesting sights to see out the window as we travelled across India from South East to North West, mostly through rolling agricultural landscape but also some cities crowded up against the tracks. It was a long day but interesting enough then I settled down for a second night on the train and finally arrived Bombay at 9am, eighteen hours after leaving Raichur. The Gothic style Victoria Terminus Station is an impressive sight in itself.

On arriving in Bombay, I booked into a hotel near the train station. A bustling market nearby sold colourful cloth of all descriptions and attracted tourists and commuters to its stalls. I had a day to spare before catching my flight to Heathrow the following morning. I hired a car and driver and braved the chaotic traffic in order to visit the main sights such as the giant rock arch named, the Gateway to India, the Taj Mahal Palace Hotel, the Parsi Towers of Silence, where the Parsis leave their dead for the vultures to devour, and Chowpatty Beach. It was a good way to see the city and spend the day rather than get bombarded by sales pitches as you wander the busy streets.

I did some mega shopping for gifts to take home. Then I had an excellent last meal and a short night at the hotel before taking a taxi to the airport for my 4.30am flight to Heathrow via Dubai. The plan was to spend two weeks in England at my sister's farm before returning to Canada. I needed to go to Cambridge for debriefing with Action Health. I wanted time to visit with my father and sister and family. I had promised Pradeep that I would try and set up charities in UK and in Canada to fund-raise for Samuha so I needed to meet with several people to facilitate that. Narayanswamy was also still in England so we planned to meet while I was there.

I was met at Heathrow by my nephew Tim. It was lovely to see all the green of England as we travelled through pretty villages to my sister's farm in Hertforshire. My sister Helen and I greeted each other with big hugs but she was horrified to see how thin I was. She said it looked as though I'd just got out of Belsen concentration camp. I could close my hand around my biceps so I knew I was thin but when I got on her scale, I found I'd lost 20 lbs. No wonder I was tired and I think I was a bit anaemic too and lacking in vitamin D. Over the next while I ate freely including lots of meat so gradually improved my health but I had lost muscle. I visited my father whose health was failing but it was good to be with him again and to go for a walk through the woods. I mostly relaxed over the next few days but then needed to plan my week-end trip to Cambridge to visit Action Health and arrange visits with previous Action Health volunteers to try and facilitate a charity for Samuha.

After a day of interviews and debriefing there, Narayanswamy came back with me to the farm. It seemed so strange to see him transplanted into this culture. We discussed charity forms but no-one in England had stepped forward to take this on. However Helen and some others in her village, offered to help with fund-raising. The following evening I drove Narayanswamy to the train station for him to return to

Birmingham, where he was taking his course. We bid each other farewell and agreed that I would most likely return to India after a year to help further develop the CBR program, but this time just for six weeks. This would be independent of Action Health, as they would continue to send health professional trainers for six month contracts. Narayanswamy still had Uganda to look forward to.

I had a lovely week of visiting family and a trip up to London to the theatre. We visited the Bury Gardens, which is adjacent to my sister's farm, and is the ancestral home of the Bowes Lyons and the Queen Mother. The expansive brick building is surrounded by rhododendrons with beautiful woodlands stretching out in each direction. A few more days of visiting with family then it was time for Tim to drive me back to Heathrow for the flight back to Vancouver. My health had recovered considerably over the two weeks at the farm. Narayanswamy's visit inspired this poem.

A SPECIAL FRIEND

Glistening teeth and a beautiful smile
Are the first impressions that beguile.
Together with the gentlest nature
Make him a friend you want to nurture.

His integrity is beyond question.
All look up to him with deep affection.
A natural leader in a gentle way,
He gives all under him a part to play.

He works with those with special needs.
Love and understanding pervade his deeds.
He strives for perfection in all that he does.
He achieves his goals without any fuss.

A teller of stories is his fame
But they are never told quite the same.
Wherever he is there's always laughter
And everyone's load is lightened after.

Ch 15
FITTING IN BACK IN CANADA

"Where you are born should not dictate your potential as a human being." Romeo Dallaire

Floyd picked me up at the Prince George airport & it was wonderful to be hugged and feel so welcomed back. I gave him a nice Indian shirt and corduroy pants, which I'd bought him as a gift.

We chatted in the car on the 50 km drive home, catching up on our news and gathering glimpses of our separate activities. Floyd curled all Winter in several different leagues. He also had a backhoe which he used to plough, not only our driveway but the old ranger station and several other properties in the community too. When the forest service moved out of the community in the eighties, we bought the ranger property which comprised of five houses, a large workshop and the post-office. We rented out the houses so now that it was Spring, Floyd was busy with maintenance there. He was still working for Westcoast Energy, a gas transmission company, based out of the Prince George office.

I asked him, "Did you learn to cook while I was away?"
"Not really", he replied. "I cooked the odd egg and had lots of cereal and toast but Brenda looked after me well and several neighbours invited me for suppers."
His job involved quite a bit of travelling too, so he could also grab meals on the road.

He asked me, “What would you like as a welcome home gift?”
I thought for a moment and quickly replied, “A computer!”
“A computer,” he said “Are you sure you can’t manage without one of those?”
“No,’ I said. “I never thought I would need one but now I do.”

We decided to just get a word processor as that was all I needed for writing reports and such. Internet still was not available. Floyd also fixed up his trail bike for me so I could feel comfortable riding our country roads. These were two items I had never really wanted before but since India, I now felt I couldn’t manage without them! I wrote this poem for Floyd.

FLOYD

Born on the farm, a Saskatchewan boy
Harnessing his siblings - a favourite ploy!
The first born of five, he grew up strong
His genetics ensured he was seldom wrong!

A strong work ethic and play hard too
Never short of a project to do
Built a couple of boats and flew his own plane
Also a ski jump for his tricks of fame

Built two log cabins, a house and a shop
Sometimes he didn’t know when to stop
Conserves water with a great passion
All kinds of waste, he’d like to ration

Started off as a Tory – committed, true blue
But now he believes the Greens are more true
He tries to teach kids the value of work
Helps them through with a financial perk

Family ski trips to Jasper each year
Memories of Mexico we also hold dear.
Curling in winter four times a week
Always competitive, he seldom is meek!

Fishing and hunting – he loves to be out
The back-roads and trails he stealthily scouts
Not a year has gone by without meat in the freezer
He really is an all-round great geezer!

His personality fills every space
No-one can keep up with his frenzied pace
Floyd, you are unique – one of a kind
Willing to help others out, in a bind

One of the first days back in Canada, I took my kayak out of storage and revelled in the peace and tranquility of a slow paddle round our Summit Lake bay, only interrupted by the haunting call of the loon. The shore-line is heavily forested with spruce, willows and birch and is a haven for moose, beaver, loons, eagles and numerous birds. One day as I was paddling I looked back and saw a bear swimming across the lake behind me. It is also quite common to see otters cavorting along, both in winter over the snow and in summer, in the creeks and lake-shore.

I reflected how back in India it was rare to get any time to oneself. Even in my hut, anyone could come in anytime and ask for a bandage or paracetamol or whatever else might be needed. Sometimes I found this frustrating but back in Summit Lake, I loved it if I bumped into anyone on the trail or on the water. Otherwise I spent much of my day in solitude, which gave me plenty of time for reflection on my time in India.

After a few days I planted the garden and returned to work at the hospital. It didn't take long to resume my normal life in Summit Lake. I thought of Babumiya, how was he doing with his recent back injury? Would he be able to walk again and if not, how would he and his family manage? I vividly remembered seeing him lying on the road surrounded by villagers. He relied on me to take control of the situation. Although I may have sounded confident, I was thinking, "How on earth can we transport Babumiya without further damaging his spine? Thank goodness I'd practiced some First Aid but this was miles from anywhere and no-one but Babumiya could speak English. We had to transport him by train to Bangalore for specialised services.

Oh the trains. I reflected on what a huge part they played in life in India. They were the most efficient way of travelling from A to B but it took ten hours to travel from the village of Jalahalli to Bangalore, a distance of 350 km. It was a microcosm of Indian life as I watched families set out a cloth on their seat and unwrap their aromatic food which would sustain them for their long journey. Sheep and goats grazed on the sparse short stubble while rocky outcroppings towered above the fields. Cotton, rice, sugar cane and sunflowers were amongst the most recognisable crops while coconut palms, mango, neem and papaya trees grew wherever there was enough moisture to sustain them.

Our family was used to going on a luxury holiday to Mexico or to Hawaii for a couple of weeks each winter. After living in India and seeing how the majority of the world live, I just couldn't do this anymore.

I said to Floyd,
"I can't go on a timeshare holiday anymore. I just don't feel right and I would feel guilty the whole time I was there. It's not right to enjoy that luxury when there are so many others who don't even know how to afford their next day's food."

He was surprised but said, "OK if that's how you feel. I don't really want to fly anymore anyway as it uses up so much fossil fuel so you'd better try and sell our timeshare." We cancelled our time-share and spent more of our time on family camping and ski trips.

When I returned to Summit Lake and to the Prince George Hospital, many colleagues asked me about my experiences in India. I loved talking about it but I knew that my colleagues couldn't really feel the power of these experiences. I missed my new friends back in India. Although I was an outsider there, could only speak English and was a visible minority, they always went out of their way to include me by switching languages partway through sentence. In fact many of them were from neighbouring States so instead of Kannadda, spoke Telegu or Tamil and conversations could be struck in multiple languages but I could usually get the gist of it.

I kept up a correspondence with Naraynswamy and he let me know how the people and the project were progressing. This was long before email so we corresponded by snail mail.

One devastating mail I received from him started,
"This will be a big surprise to you that five days ago Chandamma committed suicide by poison after she went home after work."
Chandamma was the disability worker who I had helped when she was bitten by a snake and she later travelled with me to assess people with fluorosis in a neighbouring area of Karnataka. She had been suffering from some personal problems prior to this sad event. Understandably her suicide affected Samuha and Narayanswamy really badly and they had great difficulty in accepting this.

I missed Narayanswamy's camaraderie and all the confidences we had shared. He told me about his earlier life, how he was raised on a silk farm, where they raised mulberry bushes, which fed the worms, which produced the silk, which they sold to the factory. He wore the traditional home-spun dhoti most of his early life then he became Christian and now he is non-religious but still has high morals and ethics. He is still a strong admirer of Gandhi and all that he stood for.

Juliette and others kept in touch through letters. As it turned out, Babumiya was not able to walk on discharge but he did have a little movement in his legs. He had some movement in one hand. This time he was moved in a wheelchair, making the train journey much easier. Samuha provided him and his wife with a room on the campus so he could have better care rather than return to his village. One of the disability workers spent many hours daily helping him with his exercises and helped him with his personal care. Gradually, as the weeks went by, Babumiya slowly regained his strength. He stood for the first time, six months after his accident. After three more months, he returned to his village with a wheelchair. He continued with his exercises and after eighteen months was able to walk independently.

Pradeep, the founder of Samuha, had already asked me to set up a charity in Canada to support Samuha's work. His hope was that Samuha would eventually get Canadian International Development Association, CIDA, funding. Initially ActionAid was their main sponsor but Action Aid had a ten year limit and then they pulled out of Southern India and moved North. After that Samuha secured funding from Foster Plan International but sustainable funding is always an issue. I agreed to look into funding for the disability program when I returned to Canada.

I started researching how to set up a charity to support Samuha's work. I gave a slide show on India both in Summit Lake and at the Prince George Hospital. There was lots of interest but still there was so much that just stayed inside me. I talked to some of my closest colleagues about the possibility of setting up a charity or non-profit society in Prince George to support this work. Four colleagues felt strongly enough to support me in this. Sheila Fleming, head of the physio department, immediately came on board, as the secretary. She was the one who had arranged for me to have a year's leave of absence from work to go to India in the first place and her father had made a significant donation to enable me to get there. Anne-Marie Draper, head of the occupational therapy department at the hospital also came on board, as Treasurer. Physiotherapists, Jean Tilt and Jackie Collins also joined.

A friend of Jean's, Emma Lagerstrom, joined us a little later. She worked in the International Program at the College of New Caledonia in Prince George and had previous experience writing up proposals with Hope International so she was a great help to us. Emma helped us to apply for Society status through the BC Society's Act. This was quite a simple procedure. We had already chosen our executive.

We chose our name to be Samuha Overseas Development Association. We wanted to use the word Samuha so it was clear that was our focus. We also wanted to have a catchy acronym so I thought S.O.D.A. would be appropriate and easy to remember. That is how most people remember us today.

We then needed a constitution and Bylaws. We decided to follow the Society's Act Bylaws so just needed to draw up our constitution, which stated;

The purposes of SODA are:

1. To address the annually identified needs of people with disability in the villages of South India by providing funds for corrective surgery, mobility equipment and orthotic and prosthetic supplies.
2. To reduce poverty of disabled people and their families in these villages by funding vocational, income and employment generation programs.
3. To ensure the continued quality of rehabilitation services by providing training sessions for the community based rehabilitation team in South India and by the arrangement of rehabilitation student practicums from Canada.

Any fund-raising body needs to register with the Societys Act so this was preliminary before applying for charitable status years later. We received our non-profit society status by Fall 1996.

On my last day in Bombay at the end of my fourteen months away, I had bought lots of gifts to bring home. I bought much more than I needed as I thought I could sell some of them to raise money for the disability program. I bought silk scarves, ear-rings and bangles, embroidered cotton waist-coats, Rajasthani embroidered wall-hangings and table-runners as well as some cotton table-cloths. These all just fit in my large back-pack.

Our small group of colleagues decided to hold our first fund-raising event at the Indian restaurant in Prince George called, The Taj. We did this in October 1995. We invited all the physios and occupational therapists as well as the doctors and our individual groups of friends. The restaurant had a seating capacity for sixty. We spoke to the owner, Mohammed, who was actually from Bangladesh and he was delighted. He already often catered to Doctor's functions at the Hospital and he was excited to hear that some of them were invited. It was a good way for him to promote his restaurant as well as an appropriate venue for our first Indian dinner fundraiser. We bargained for a fair price for a set dinner so we would make a profit for our society and Mohammed would still make a profit for his restaurant. He would also get all the profits from the bar, as drinks were not included in the price of a ticket. We decided to charge $20.00/ticket, which included a $5.00 donation per dinner to S.O.D.A.

In 1995 we reasoned this was a fair price for a good dinner plus a donation. Mohammed set aside one table for us to sell some of the items I'd brought back from India. Our selling price was double what I had paid in India and we thought this produced bargains for our guests.

Just the aroma of the food emanating from the restaurant was enough to entice anyone with a generous spirit and transport them to the Indian culture. Mohammed cooked us onion pakoras, as appetisers, followed by chapattis, vegetable jalfreezi, palak paneer, dahl, butter chicken and lamb curry. It was all delicious and served buffet style. It was much enjoyed by everyone. Mohammed animatedly chatted with all the doctors and others, who he recognised. He was very happy to host this event. He also had traditional rice pudding and wickedly sweet gulab jammon for desserts. He supplied Indian Kingfisher beer as well as an assortment of other drinks and traditional chai. The décor of the restaurant is authentic with tables set in small cubicles and plants draped over the dividers. Quiet tonal music in the background and a large sculpted metal orb by the entrance complete the ambiance.

We had to move the planters and some other decorations to enable people to see the screen for the slide-show. This is really the most important part of the evening as guests see the transformation of young children crawling or hopping through their village on their deformed legs. Then comes the therapy, which includes stretching and casting of the deformed limbs before the application of the custom braces and supplying them with crutches. They see the broad smiles, spread across the children's faces as they stand and walk for the first time and stand at eye level with their peers. Some guests, including Floyd, shed tears and they all reach deeper into their pockets to donate to help this program. The restaurant buzzed with animated conversation as people got to chat with friends, they may not have seen for many months, while discussing the virtues of the program.

During the slide show, we told them how every cent raised goes to help the children and families with disability as I pay for my own flight and we cover our own overheads such as postage, printing and other costs. At this first fund-raising dinner we collected a profit of $750.00, which we thought was quite encouraging. Forty people came to the dinner and I was happy to report back to Pradeep that we had achieved this much. Those that came out to the dinner and who saw the slides were very impressed with all the work that Samuha was doing. I also told them of my plans for returning to India in the Fall of 1996 to help expand the program into Koppal District and to train a small new team of disability workers.

We continued to give slide-shows and talks about Samuha to small community groups and we set up a table to sell the purchases from India at work, at my church and at some community gatherings. Gradually the word got out about Samuha and the good work they are doing. The Prince George Citizen wrote an article in the local paper about "Local physiotherapist goes to India to work with children with Polio."

I told Narayanswamy about our efforts.
"Forty people came to the dinner and they paid $20.00 each, $5.00 of which was profit for Samuha."
"$20.00!" he said, amazed. "Why would anyone pay that much for dinner? Here it only costs us the equivalent of 2c for a cup of tea. $2.00 for a full meal would be considered expensive. That's amazing that you could charge so much and people were willing to pay!"

Ch 16
SAMUHA OVERSEAS DEVELOPMENT ASSOCIATION

"Courage my friends, 'tis not too late to build a better world." Tommy Douglas

As Fall approached, we became busy harvesting the garden, making pickles, freezing and canning the fruits and vegetables. This also involved picking the apples for juice and picking pails of huckleberries for winter use and jam.

I also went hunting with Floyd and after we got our moose and hung it for a couple of weeks, he butchered it while I wrapped it for the freezer. These hunting trips were always good fun as we took our river boat up the river and stayed in an old trapper's cabin. It usually took a few days of hiking through the bush to various swamps before we found and shot our moose, then the hard work began. I helped Floyd dress it out, quarter it and skin it. We usually hung it in a tree overnight so it firmed up before we packed the quarters on to our backs, tied to pack-boards, and packed the meat out to the river where we loaded it on to our boat. Floyd cut a trail with his chain-saw from the kill to the river so we wouldn't have to climb over too many wind-fall logs to get it out but it was still a struggle. He always tried to shoot within a kilometer of shore so that was our maximum length of pack.

We then drove our boat back to where we had left our truck and trailer. We winched the boat up on to the trailer then drove slowly hauling the heavy but precious load back home where we hung the quarters in a cool basement for another two weeks. We also made our own sausages from all the trimmings, usually about 200 lb of sausages, which our daughter Brenda came and helped with as we needed about four of us to feed the grinder, guide the meat into skins, twist them into sausages and wrap them. This was one aspect of my life that I hadn't shared with anyone in India as they were mostly vegetarian and didn't approve of killing animals.

In India I worked hard and long hours training the team and providing therapy to the kids and gradually expanding the program but once that work was done each day, I was free to read or enjoy evenings in Mahesh's hut or go for walks.

Back home though, it was a full-time job just to live. I worked three days a week at the hospital but on top of that I planted, weeded, harvested and preserved the garden and mowed the lawn. I made all the meals and kept the house as clean as I could and did the weekly laundry. We cooked and heated the house with wood, which Floyd split and hauled. He was still working too and did the repairs on the vehicles and any home repairs that were needed. We also collected our drinking water from the spring each month, 20 km down the road.

In India, different members of staff do all these jobs. They cooked our meals, we washed our own plates. We swept out our hut but staff kept the grounds neat and tidy and hauled the drinking water for us. Several villagers grew more fruit and vegetables than they could eat so they brought all their extras to the weekly market so Samuha always had an abundant supply of fresh vegetables. This method ensured that as many people as possible had enough work to sustain their families.

Right after Christmas I had a phone call from my sister saying that our father was ill and I should fly home. I arranged my flight as soon as I could but I arrived there a few hours after he had passed away. My father had always told me, "Take every opportunity that comes your way." This advice stuck with me and probably contributed to my decision to travel overseas to India. I stayed at the farm for the funeral and family visits. I also visited Juliette in London. She had completed her six months with Samuha and had returned home to London. It was good to catch up on Samuha's news. After a couple of weeks I returned to Canada and continued working at the hospital.

Summit Lake is a small community of about ten families which expands in Summer when people come out from neighbouring communities to enjoy their cabins. The permanent residents are mostly retired as, since the saw-mills closed, there is no employment any longer in Summit Lake. The school closed as did the post-office. The store and gas station burnt down and the restaurant was pulled down to make room for campers. This means there aren't any young people we could call on for help with heavy tasks. We are often called on to shovel rooves for others in the winter. We don't mind doing this to keep fit but sometimes it cuts into recreation time.

Winter is our quiet time, once the garden is harvested and the meat is in the freezer. I love cross-country skiing through the trails in the forest. Sometimes I feel as though I am the only person in the community and I often am. I can see all the activities of the previous day or night by following the tracks in the snow. I see that a moose has followed my tracks of the previous day and then has bedded down close to the trail. A grouse has flown into the deep snow and buried itself there to keep warm overnight. Coyote and rabbit tracks criss-cross in the snow with the rabbits making a broad solid trail in some places.

As I ski along and notice these stories in the snow, I ponder about the heat in India. How we travelled to the village early in the morning and late in the evening to avoid the heat and to find the families at home before they went to the fields to work. How we always chose a place in the shade to do our work.

I still felt uncomfortable when we went into new villages, where no westerners had been before. They just stared at me without blinking, sometimes the children would start giggling and occasionally poke at me or pull my hair then run away. It was most disconcerting but it made me reflect how foreigners must sometimes feel in our country.

While skiing along the trail I remembered Virupakshi and wondered how he was managing. He was four years old when I met him and had severe polio of one leg and also some paralysis in his other leg. We spent many weeks with therapy to enable him to walk. He should be ready to attend school soon.

I also thought of Prabhu. I remembered travelling by motorbike to give him his daily injections. "I hope no-one in Canada will give me trouble for giving intra-muscular injections, definitely outside my scope of practice, but who will know and what choice did I have?" "I wonder how Prabhu is doing now? Will he fully recover? Is he still in his body cast?"

I kicked and glided absent-mindedly further into the forest. I started thinking about Narayanswamy. He was an engaging man of marrying age. "Had he found a suitable female yet or was he still looking?" "Would he choose anyone from Samuha staff? Will he have a happy marriage and family? I hope so, as he will make a wonderful father."

I came to a fork in the trail and decided to ski down towards the lake then round the shoreline back home. When I reached the shore there, on the opposite side of the lake, was a cow and calf moose browsing on the willows. They didn't hear me quietly gliding along the fluffy snow so I stayed and watched them until they slowly ambled into the trees and out of sight.

I continued around the shore until I could see our home with our light shining through the trees. I thought how lucky I was to live here in this comparative wilderness. Opposite our house was an island, which the kids sometimes swam to and pretended it was Hawaii. It was a far cry from Hawaii now with the snow hanging from the trees and the clear crisp air caused frost to build up on my eyebrows. I climbed up our trail from the lake to the house revelling in the peaceful couple of hours I had spent, alone with my thoughts, as I wandered through the trees.

India is 13 ½ hours ahead of us here in Western Canada. My colleagues would be rising for the start of their day and early morning cup of tea pretty soon as they usually get up at 6am. As soon as I get home now, I will stoke up the fire, tidy up the house then start preparing supper. Floyd should be home in an hour or two. I already shovelled the snow from the driveway this morning and Floyd filled the wood box with wood before he went to work. We might even have time for a game of backgammon. We had got over our differences and enjoyed each other's company.

It snowed heavily overnight so the next morning I started shovelling the driveway with the wide scoop-shovel. It took three attempts just to clear a route from the house to the top of the bank, where I could push the snow over the bank towards the lake. Once I got this first trail cleared, the rest became easier as I could push each shovel load along the same trail and over the bank. The job can get quite tedious and takes a couple of hours usually but again this routine activity gave me a chance to ponder my Indian experiences.

This time I thought of Ayyamma at ten years old. I was amazed how she travelled on her own for treatment of her club-foot every two weeks on the bus from Tinthinni, about two hours away from the Jalahalli clinic. I wondered how she was doing. She was determined to walk without a limp so her marriage chances would be better. I remembered how she was always wearing the same yellow dress. "Was this the only dress she had or was it her best dress, which she wore to come to Samuha? Will she find a good match for a husband in a few years or will her family marry her off at an early age to an older man, as is so often the custom."

Arranged marriages may not be so bad if the parents of both partners research the family background and look for common interests. Love marriages don't always work out either, I thought. What is bad though is child marriage when the family marry off their daughter, often to a much older man and as soon as the girl reaches puberty, she has to move into her husband's home. These girls don't have a chance to complete their education so have no means of supporting themselves if they want to leave the marriage. If life becomes unbearable they either commit suicide or have to prostitute themselves as their family won't usually take them back. Thank goodness we have options here to make sure we have happy and productive lives. I ponder the differences and am thankful that I have made Samuha part of my life but I can continue to live in Canada.

Before the end of March, it finally stopped snowing but there were still several feet of snow on the ground. As the temperature warmed, helped by some showers, the snow gradually melted so that we could start digging over the garden. We raked all the fallen leaves and sticks off the lawn so it could also recover. At the end of April I started planting the vegetables but it was still too cold and damp for some seeds such as beans and the tomato plants. We usually try and have the whole garden planted by the end of May so that the vegetables have time to mature before the frosts start again in October. It is a short growing season but all the root crops do well as do peas, beans, cabbage and broccoli. Tomatoes and cucumbers have to be covered at the beginning and end of season to protect them from the cold.

Apart from gardening and working, I mowed the lawn with our little push-mower. Most of our summer recreation time was spent kayaking on the lake but just the activities of daily living kept us both busy. A good deal of time at home was also spent building and promoting S.O.D.A.

Once we receive our non-profit society status, we consider how we can increase our fund-raising activities. Emma suggested,
"We could ask Hope International if they will issue tax receipts for our donors. In this way donors will be inclined to give more generously."
We thought this was a good idea and Emma agreed to apply to Hope on our behalf.

The reply back from them was,
"Yes, we would be happy to issue tax receipts for your donors. We will take ten percent of the donation for Hope and the rest will go to Samuha."
We thought this was a fair exchange and that it should still enable us to increase our funds so we agreed to the arrangement.

Our S.O.D.A. committee all worked full or part-time so we had limited time we could dedicate to raising funds for Samuha. We decided that one fund-raising dinner each Fall should be our main activity. We would also speak to schools or other community groups to raise awareness, as requested. We needed to record accurate minutes and financial transactions to comply with the Societys Act. We also started collecting names and addresses of donors for future dinners and activities. From these modest beginnings, we gradually built a network of friends and followers to support Samuha's work.

We continued to meet monthly and printed some brochures to explain the purposes of our group. For our next dinner, which we also held at the Taj, we put invitations in all the doctors' mail-boxes and handed them out to all the physio clinics in town as well as put posters up in the Hospital, Library, Church and public notice boards. We notified all the media and invited CBC and the Prince George Citizen to the dinner. The Citizen did an interview prior to the event and gave us good publicity with a full page article and photo of Siddappa being carried to the clinic on his grandfather's shoulders.

Mohammed again put on a superb dinner for us. I dressed in one of my Indian outfits and all the guests came smartly dressed for the occasion. Again we put on a slide-show and this time concentrated on the children with club-feet as there were several orthopaedic surgeons in the audience.

I explained,
"We correct the feet by stretching and applying serial casts. We change the cast every two weeks until we have fully corrected the position, then we apply a foot splint which the child is instructed to wear daily. They are also taught stretching and strengthening exercises. We continue to follow them for another year to make sure the correction is maintained."
One of the surgeons interjected,
"There's no way you could correct the club-foot conservatively if the child has already been walking on the deformed foot. If you took an x-ray, you would see that the bones and joints are still out of position."

I replied,
"The children have never been x-rayed before or after the procedure. That is too expensive for the families. The family's concern is to make the foot look normal and reduce or remove the limp so the child can lead a normal active life. They don't mind what the foot looks like on x-ray as long as the child can walk to school and work in the field and not be ostracised by anyone."

We saw several children in India who had had surgical correction of their foot but they hadn't received any splinting or follow-up, so the deformity returned. We found that it was impossible to manually correct these deformities so we had to send these children back to the surgeon for release of the scar tissue. Then we made a splint for the child to wear and showed them corrective exercises so the deformity would not return again. In Canada, clubfoot is corrected immediately after birth and splinted so by the time the child is ready to weight-bear, they have a normal appearing foot.

Again there was great camaraderie at the dinner. Forty six people came and we made a profit of $1,000.00. These were very modest beginnings but those that came enjoyed the evening and were impressed by the work and gradually word started to spread.

I continued to communicate with Pradeep and Narayanswamy. They wanted to expand the program into Koppal, another area of Karnataka. They asked me if I would return to Samuha to provide training to a new small team of disability workers to get this new program off the ground. I was certainly interested in returning there but this time for a shorter period. I arranged to take six weeks' vacation from the hospital in October through November. Floyd was in full agreement with this plan. This was a good time to be away from Canada, after the garden had been harvested, and a cool time to be in India. Little did I know then that this would become a pattern of six week visits over the next several years as both SODA and Samuha grew exponentially.

Shortly after the dinner I started preparing for this next visit to India. Two of the trainees had no knowledge of community based rehabilitation but Pranesh, who was to be team leader, already had some experience. I collected my training notes and prepared the first few lesson plans. I packed my Indian clothing, some pens and small gifts of T-shirts and ball hats for the CBR workers and Samuha staff. I booked my flights from Vancouver to Delhi and on to Bangalore.

We still needed to harvest our Summit Lake garden and preserve the produce for winter. We harvested and stored half of our carrots and potatoes in our cold room. The rest we left in the ground, protected by bags of leaves, so they wouldn't freeze before the snow came to protect them. I pickled beets and made lots of strawberry, rhubarb and raspberry jam. We picked gallons of huckleberries, which I froze in small containers. Floyd helped me pick the apples, which I then made into juice for canning. He was going to have to hunt and butcher the moose himself as I would be away for that process.

Once all this was done, I acquired sufficient money in travellers' cheques to last me six weeks and obtained the required anti-malarial prescription. I carried the $1,000.00 cheque for Samuha with me, the proceeds we had made from our dinner, which I would give to Narayanswamy when I arrived in Bangalore.

Before I left, I prepared a few meals for Floyd and packaged them in the freezer then we hugged and said our "good-byes," both to him and to family and friends.

Six weeks was a comparatively short time and didn't seem nearly as disruptive to family life. Floyd drove me to the Prince George airport. He still had his hunting to look forward to and I was excited to be seeing my new Indian friends and family again. We arranged that Floyd would meet me at Heathrow in December then we'd both go to my sister's farm in England for a couple of weeks before flying home to Canada in time for Christmas.

PART 2

ANNUAL TRIPS TO INDIA WITH EVOLUTION OF SAMUHA AND S.O.D.A.

17
RETURN TO INDIA TO SET UP KOPPAL, OCTOBER 1996.

"Nothing About Us Without Us" David Werner

In Delhi, I woke to the sound of the call to prayer followed by honking horns of traffic and the smells of spices and urine permeating the air. The journey took two nine-hour flights from Vancouver with a few hours delay at Heathrow airport. After the long journey, I collapsed for the night in Delhi at a smart hotel and had a good rest.

The following morning I took a taxi across the city to the domestic airport through air thick with acrid fumes. I remembered my trepidation when I first arrived two years earlier. This time I was no longer hesitant to trust my welfare to the taxi-driver. I took the local scenes and aromas in stride. The locals had scarves tied across their mouths and noses, obviously to combat the pollution, which was so thick from all the exhausts, particularly from the 2-stroke auto-rickshaws. I had grown a lot in the two years since I had first arrived in India, when I was so full of fear and trepidation.

My next flight was from Delhi to Bangalore and I was happy to be met at the airport there by Pradeep and Narayanswamy. We drove to Pradeep's house by jeep, where he had arranged a party for most of the Sector Heads of Samuha. It was so good to meet up with everyone again and enjoy a social gathering. The home was simply decorated with large cushions on the floor and low tables for eating off. The walls were white with red and orange cloth draped strategically. He had shelves overflowing with books and I was surprised to find a book in his library written by a friend of mine from England, Andrew Osmond, called Scotch on the Rocks, a political satire. It is amazing how connections are made across the miles.

I stayed overnight at Pradeep's. The next morning, Narayanswamy & I visited Hema, the lady with disability who had founded the Association for the Physically Handicapped, APH, in Bangalore. Hema was always inspiring, having achieved so much to improve the lives of people living with disability in India. She also attended international conferences and helped to create awareness and change mind-sets around disability. She had a bubbly personality and was an influential person on the Board of Samuha. We discussed some future plans for Samuha, including instigation of a horticulture program. I spent one more night in Bangalore at the Vellara Hotel then took the overnight train up to Raichur and on to Jalahalli.

As usual, it was like coming home when we drove through the gates of the campus as everyone came out smiling to greet us. Yael Levy had returned as the physio trainer. She was the first Action Health volunteer physiotherapist who went to Samuha in 1992 and she decided to return for a further six months. I stayed in Jalahalli for one week before heading to Koppal to start the project there. I concentrated that week on developing the training manuals.

It was wonderful to be greeted by Babaumiya, smiling and standing independently.
“Babumiya, it is so good to see you and how well you are doing!”
“Namaksara Madam. I am so thankful and so happy to see you.” He replied.

I performed a muscle chart on him to assess his recovery from his spinal cord injury and to determine what work he would be able to do. Muscle strength is graded on five levels, where 5, is normal strength and 1, is just a flicker of movement. Progress can be accurately determined by plotting these results on a chart for each muscle group and suitable strengthening exercises can be devised from these results. Babumiya’s upper limbs were fine except for mild weakness of his left hand. His hip muscles were now pretty good, all grade 4, but his right knee muscles could barely straighten against gravity and his right ankle muscles were too weak to lift his foot against gravity, only grade 2, hence his foot drop on the right. He was now just beginning to walk without a walker.

“Babumiya, you should be able to help in the clinics and assess children and write up the needed reports. Your right hand strength has improved considerably and since most of the charting is done on the computer, it requires less hand strength than gripping a pen so you should manage.”
“Yes, Madam, I think I can do that. Thanks you Madam.”

Babumiya continued with his strengthening exercises and his walking became progressively easier but he still had a foot-drop on the right causing him to walk with a limp.

While I was still in Jalahalli, I reported on SODA to the Samuha Board to let them know that we had established a non-profit society in Canada, which they were pleased to hear. Some people in England had also agreed to do some fund-raising but they didn't have a formal society. My sister, Helen Roberts, and Geoff Duncan, the father of Ruth, an Action Health speech therapist, both raised some considerable funds for Samuha in England through their different networks.

In October, we finally drove to Koppal. Narayanswamy had recruited Pranesh, who was to run the program there and two new disability workers, Virupakshi Alawandi and Shivanappa Hakki. We immediately visited some villages to assess several children and to introduce ourselves to the village organisers. It is important to build trust and goodwill in the community so the elders and families understand the purpose of our visits and co-operate with suggestions for their childrens' progress. We were still working mostly with polio as well as some children with club feet.

Our clinic was in a flat roofed house on the edge of town. A local girl and I shared one room, where we rolled our mats down on the floor each night for sleeping. There was a small office and a larger assessment room for one or two families to bring their children. Nearly all the orthotic work, such as fitting of wheelchairs and casting, was done outdoors. A small kitchen and a bathroom completed the amenities. It wasn't nearly as nice as living on campus but it was alright just for a month or so.

We ate our meals outside and when we washed off our plates at the outdoor tap, the black long-haired pigs came running to eat up any scraps. Pigs act as a host for the mosquito in the transmission of Japanese Encephalitis. I had never been vaccinated against this disease as the vaccine was quite expensive and not totally effective, which was a worry. The water quality and quantity was marginal there. This was another region where there were high levels of fluoride in the ground water.

Narayanswamy stayed with us in Koppal for a couple of days and the routine became village visits by day and training sessions in the evening. The basement of the house conveniently served as a training hall. Pranesh had already undergone some of the training and Virupakshi was quick to learn. Hakki found it a bit more difficult but he went on to become an assistant orthotic technician so he could help make the braces for children with polio.

One of the children we saw on these village visits was Balavva in the village of Tigari. She was six years old and had polio affecting both of her legs. Her family had made a wooden trolley, which her brothers used, to pull her the two kilometres to school. Her hips and knees were fixed at over 90 degrees flexion and both her ankles were fixed pointing down. She could only move around by crawling on her hands and knees. She had contracted polio before she learned to walk so had never walked.

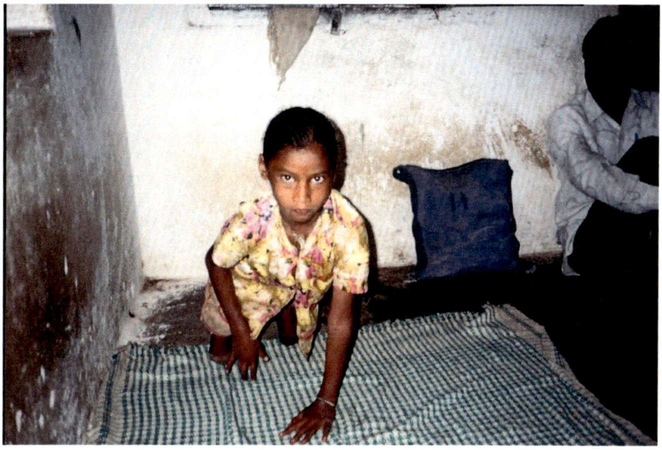

Balavva 1996

Virupakshi explained to the family how they needed to stretch her joints daily and he would apply plaster casts next time he came, to straighten her legs as much as possible. After a few weeks of this, she would need to go to Bangalore for corrective surgery then she would have to wear leg braces and use crutches to walk. The family listened and agreed to help their daughter by following these instructions. It took several months to complete this process but then Balavva at least had a chance in life. It was good that they were already helping her to get to school daily so she could receive her education.

The training sessions covered the principles of community based rehabilitation, general anatomy, principles of polio, how to measure joint range and muscle strength, how to decide whether surgery is needed and the principles of casting. They were also taught how to build parallel bars for gait training and how to make and fit calipers and splints. We had already completed a training manual on polio and club foot so they had this for a resource. Pranesh was a competent leader so after four weeks of training, I felt confident that they would be able to carry on this work. They also had Narayanswamy and the rest of the team to help them. After a couple of days in Koppal, Narayanswamy returned to Jalahalli.

Kukinoor, who ran the rest of the Koppal Samuha project, Pranesh and I drove to a large Temple in a neighbouring village one evening, where they celebrated the Dussehra Festival with a large elephant procession, which was awesome to see. The elephants were decorated and the Mahuts wore gaily coloured costumes and turbans as they sat proudly on their animals. It was amazing to see this in a small village but the Temple was of importance to the local area.

A few days later, Pradeep and Narayanswamy visited and we drove by jeep to a rocky area, not far from Koppal, where Pradeep wanted to set up a new Samuha campus. It was a delightful area, close to the highway but no buildings near it and it comprised of a significant rocky outcropping which you could climb and get a great view of the area. It must have suited everyone as a couple of years later the campus was built there on flat ground close to this rocky outcropping and is called Irkalgada.

I stayed in Koppal for a few more weeks doing more training and village visits. We helped families build parallel bars out of bamboo outside their homes so their child could learn to walk, once they were supplied with a leg brace. We visited schools and encouraged the teachers to accept children with disability into their school. We also initiated discussions on ramping and building of toilets in these schools to accommodate children with disability.

The day Balavva received her braces and crutches was amazing. The family had already built her a set of parallel bars so when Balavva stood up with the braces for the first time in her life and used the bars for balance, a broad grin of pure happiness spread across her face. She even started giggling. I'd never seen a girl so radiant with happiness after finding she could stand up for the first time in her life at the age of six years old. It didn't take her long to learn how to walk with crutches and from that day, she never looked back.

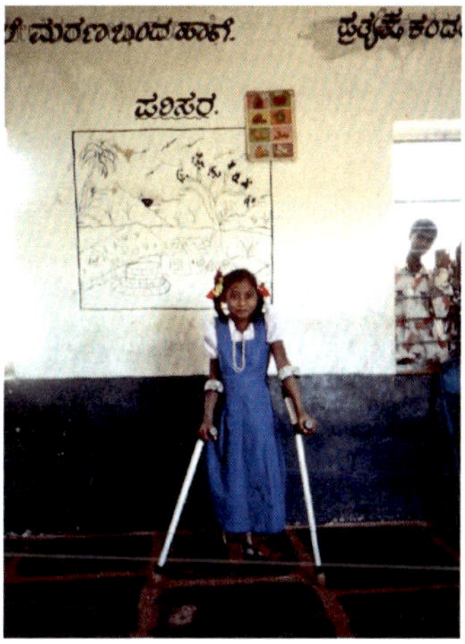

Balavva

On one visit to a more isolated village, my TVS motorbike broke down. Pranesh calmly tied a rope between his bike and my bike and we travelled a couple of kilometres over a narrow rough trail with me sitting on my bike to balance it and him steering us over the rough terrain until we reached the road and we could fix my bike. I would never have thought it possible but neither of us fell off and we reached our destination safely.

Narayanswamy visited again towards the end of my stay in Koppal. Pranesh organised a farewell party for me up on the roof of the house with music and singing. He also organised a picnic in Hampi, which we all enjoyed, sitting on the rocks in the river while we ate. We watched coracle boats ply people across the river and absorbed the tranquil life as buffalo wallowed in the water while women washed their clothes and children swam.

The next day Narayanswamy and I drove back to Jalahalli, about a four hour journey on dusty, bumpy roads. The following day was Diwali, the biggest Hindu Festival, something like our Christmas, where the girls dress up in new saris and everyone exchanges gifts and everywhere is festooned with lights. We celebrated it by having supper in Mahesh's house with oil lamps burning on the verandah. It was low-key but most pleasant.

The following day I was invited to Babumiya's home for supper. His home was off the main road and surrounded by fields. His family greeted me warmly and prepared an amazing meal of lamb curry with roti and sweets, which we ate with our fingers while sitting on the floor cross-legged. Babumiya and his family felt that I had saved him from permanent disability, when he was tossed by the bullock, but in fact Babumiya saved himself by directing his own care in the first instance, refusing to be moved until I got there.

After this, it was time to write up some reports and finish my work and prepare for leaving Jalahalli again. After a farewell party in Jalahalli I headed to Delhi and then to Heathrow. There I was met by my nephew Tim and my husband, Floyd, who had already flown into Heathrow from Canada. We enjoyed our holiday there together, staying in England for just over a week at my sister's farm.

Apart from enjoying the social scene in London, where we went to Covent Garden and to River Dance, we were also involved in some fund-raising events in Whitwell, my sister's village. I gave a talk on India to the students at Princess Helena College there and to the village primary school. On the Saturday, Helen had booked the village hall for an Auction of Promises in aid of Samuha. This is an auction where, instead of bidding on actual "things", you bid on promises, which varied from a plate of mince-pies, to a tour of the Old Bailey to a week in a cabin on Summit Lake and many more very generous offers.

The Hall filled up for this sold-out event. People were offered a glass of wine and some appetisers. I showed some slides of our work in India and gave a short talk then the auction started with my brother-in-law, Peter, being the auctioneer. Hands flew up around the room as guests competed for prizes. The bids were extremely generous and the variety of promises ensured that every participant could bid on something of interest and in their price-range. We made over $15,000.00 at this event, which was amazing and far more than we had managed to raise at any of our fund-raising dinners in Canada up to that point. All of this money was sent to Samuha to help them run their disability program.

A couple of days after the auction, Floyd and I flew back to Vancouver and after Christmas I returned to work at the Prince George Hospital. Floyd & I continued with our activities and enjoyed skiing in the winter and canoeing and gardening in the summer. Floyd retired in 1996 but continued to do some consulting work in the USA.

SODA continued with annual fund-raising dinners in Prince George and I returned annually to India to give more training to the Koppal team and to further develop the training manuals. In 1999 Action Health completed their ten year partnership with Samuha so they were no longer going to send health trainers to Samuha. I was concerned that the quality of the work might deteriorate without a professional therapy trainer on the team so I wanted to devise a system where I could continue to return to India annually to monitor the progress of the program and offer further training as needed. Gradually the idea of setting up student placements for Canadian Physiotherapy and Occupational Therapy students materialised.

18

ROTARY, CHARITY AND STUDENTS.

"Intelligence is the ability to adapt to change"

Stephen Hawking

Later that year, I registered in an on-line post-graduate diploma course on program development. I wanted to base my program on setting up student placements for Canadian therapy students in India. The course was taught by Sue Stanton, an Occupational Therapy professor at UBC. The components of this course included designing a needs assessment, preparing a budget and designing a program evaluation. I found the needs assessment component most useful.

I surveyed all the Physiotherapy and Occupational Therapy schools across Canada, both the faculty and students. I surveyed the professional associations and the licensing bodies as well as the Board of Samuha. I was surprised that all the Canadian feedback was positive. I knew the students would all be interested but I wasn't sure if the universities would accept SAMUHA as a placement site as there were no medical professionals on site, no hospital and no library. I also didn't expect the Occupational Therapy profession to accept a physiotherapist as their students' preceptor but they offered no objections. The only dissenting voice was the Board of Samuha as they felt that the disability program should be able to stand on their own two feet after the ten year partnership with Action Health. However it was agreed to run a pilot.

The plan was for me to be the preceptor for the Canadian students. We would start off with two students so they could keep each other company as well as help each other to learn. We wanted to take one physio and one occupational therapy student together each time but unfortunately the placement times didn't allow for this so we initially took two occupational therapy students from the University of Alberta. There were eleven applicants from across the country so each student had to complete a questionnaire and then the short-list was interviewed. All the applicants were of high academic standing so the choice was made more from ability for independent thinking, willingness to take risks and to accept simple living conditions.

I timed the placements for either November/December or January/ February so the climate would be tolerable in India. The first placement was to be November 2001 but unfortunately there was unrest between Pakistan and India at that time and Canada put out a travel advisory so the University wouldn't let us go. Fortunately the crisis was short-lived and the advisory was lifted by the end of the year so the students and I set off in January 2002 for our first six week placement.

Samuha had built a new campus at Jalahalli so this is where we stayed. The students lived in the women's dorm and my hut was nearby. Since my last visit, Narayanswamy had married Chitra, who was one of the social workers who had lived on the old Jalahalli campus. They now lived close to our accommodation. When I visited them one evening, Narayanswamy showed his photos from his trip to UK and Uganda. I was amused to see that these included a photograph of my sister's bathroom which contains a Victorian style bath in a large carpeted room. I had also taken photos of the bathroom at Samuha which comprised of a tiled hole in the cement floor, a tap and a bucket. The contrast was stark and it was interesting that we had both found them unique enough to photograph!

The huts on campus were all thatched and had mud floors and metal beds with thin mattresses. The bathroom was down the path and again was open–rooved and the whole campus was surrounded by trees and situated at the base of a hill, close to the highway but about two kilometres from the village. There was a dairy across the road and a tree-lined avenue led towards the village.

The two students were Tamiza Janmohamed and Leanne DeCoste. Tamiza was Ismaeli and fitted in easily to the culture. Leanne was tall with long blonde hair so stood out in a crowd of shorter, brown people. They were both excellent students and accommodated well to the program. Rural India has limited access to electricity and one morning all the power went off on campus when Tamiza plugged in her hair-dryer. She learnt fast and never did that again!

These student placements were really a win-win-win situation as it allowed me to monitor the program and provide extra training to the team. The students learnt new skills and the principles of community based rehabilitation and how to manage with minimal equipment, while the children and families benefitted from increased therapy inputs and the disability team strengthened their skills.

My goal for the Canadian students during their placements, apart from their own learning requirements, was to design a piece of adaptive equipment for a client and to leave some piece of equipment for the team which could enhance the program. Leanne designed a wrist splint with a bent spoon attached for a quadriplegic patient, who was unable to feed himself but with this splinted spoon, he could be independent with his feeding. This was his main desire and he was delighted with the result.

Tamiza designed a pill box for a client with mental health impairment, who frequently overdosed on her medication, as she forgot to take her pills at the prescribed time. This resulted in her taking extra pills when she remembered. Because most of these adult clients weren't able to read or write, Tamiza designed some match boxes glued together to contain the pills with a picture of the moon, rising sun and setting sun for the three times of day when the pills should be taken. This simple idea solved the overdosing problem and helped to maintain the client's mental health. This method was then adapted for future clients.

Mental Health is a huge problem in rural India. Medical care and prescriptions are often not available and poorly understood. We have seen some horrific examples of neglect or of lack of understanding. The worst was to see a teenage child chained to a cart by a metal ring around her neck with a length of chain attached to the cart. This was done to prevent her from wandering around the village and going into people's homes, the residents of which were complaining. She was kept chained daily. We've seen several adults with deep wounds on their legs from where they have been chained to stop them wandering. A common treatment was to place a mentally ill person on the rocks in the hot sun with a green mustard type paste stuffed up their nostrils.

Samuha provides counselling for mental health families through Manohar, who comes up from Mysore each month to help Samuha's clients. There is also a psychiatrist, Dr Ajaykumar, who helps Samuha and prescribes appropriate medicines for Samuha's clients but there are so many people who are not known to Samuha who do not have access to suitable care.

The students were expected to teach for a day each on a topic of the team's choosing. The students knew which topic they would be teaching before leaving Canada so they could bring the appropriate teaching materials with them. The disability workers acted as our interpreters in the village as they had learnt enough English to communicate the students' questions to the parents. Usually the disability workers were fluent in the family's language but not always, since the Moslems mostly spoke Urdu or Hindi whereas the majority of families spoke the local language, Kannada. On the training days, Narayanswamy or the Assistant Director, Hampanna were the translators. This meant that training sessions always took twice as long as anticipated since everything had to be translated, including all the questions and answers. We also used pictures and practical exercises as much as possible so a lot of the learning could be done without too much written work.

The students saw all kinds of conditions which they may not see in Canada, such as rickets, TB joints and of course, polio. They learned to develop methods of facilitating movement without any fancy equipment. For example we often used a sack of rice as a support to facilitate children sitting to standing or a rolled up blanket under the abdomen to enable crawling. For the first ten years we were there, we were mostly working with children with polio but this gradually changed to children with cerebral palsy, spina -bifida, malnutrition, rickets and several other conditions, as well as some adults.

Mounesh was an unfortunate child. We first met him when Kallappa took the students and I to his home in the neighbouring village, Karadigudda. He was about twelve years old and recently injured.

Kallappa asked the parents, "What happened to Mounesh?"
They replied in Kannada, "He fell off the bullock cart a week or two ago and hasn't been able to walk since."

I asked Kallappa to ask them if he could get himself up when he fell.
The answer was, “Yes, he limped home but now he can’t walk.”
I took a look at his back. There was a large protuberance over the middle of his spine. I asked Kallappa to ask if anyone in the family had TB. They looked surprised but answered, “Yes, his father had TB of his lungs. I asked the family to take Mounesh for x-rays and to get started on TB medications and we’d be back to see them the next week.

As we walked away Kallappa said, “I thought he had broken his back from the fall?”
I told him “if he had broken his back then, he wouldn’t have been able to get up and walk home and it’s not a big distance for him to fall. Once we looked at his back, you could see the typical signs of Potts Disease, which is indicative of TB. His father’s history then confirmed it. This is why taking a full history is so important.”
This was an important learning moment for both Kallappa and the students.

Mounesh did have TB of his spine but he didn’t take his medications regularly and he never had any surgical intervention. He went on to develop spasticity and paralysis of his legs. He needed to use a hand propelled tricycle to get around. Samuha built him an accessible toilet so that he didn’t have to travel out to the fields and perch on the frame of his bike to relieve himself. It is very difficult for these people who live in rural areas in South India and have a disability. There is very little help for them and unless they have access to an organization like Samuha, just ordinary tasks of everyday living become very difficult. Mounesh later ran a small shop in his village as an income generation project. I followed him for years as we always stopped in at his shop on the way by and had a chat.

Mounesh and Leanne in his village

These first Canadian students were exceptional and really valued their experience with Samuha. It was a great introduction to many more years of taking students for six week practicums to India. The Samuha staff enjoyed their interactions also. Sometimes I took occupational therapists and sometimes physiotherapists. Best of all was when I could take both disciplines together.

In 2000, I was invited to give a talk and slide-show to the Prince George Rotary club on Samuha. A couple of their members had been to one of our fund-raising dinners and were most interested to help since their goal, together with the World Health Organisation, WHO, was to eradicate polio world-wide. After my talk and slide-show, the club decided that they would indeed support Samuha's work. They agreed to fund equipment and supplies to facilitate the eradication of polio in these villages.

They provided a fridge to keep the vaccine cold as polio vaccine has to be kept colder than four degrees Celsius to be potent. The main reason that polio had not yet been eradicated was because there was no way to keep the vaccine cold in the villages. Once this was understood, WHO and Rotary concentrated on supplying fridges to keep the vaccine cold and cold boxes to transport the vaccine to the villages. Samuha's role was to mobilise their vehicles for the transportation of nurses and vaccine and to help round up all the children in the villages.

The Prince George Rotary Club funnelled their donation through International Rotary where the funds were doubled Provincially, then Nationally, then Internationally. The total donation was $80,000.00 over a two year period so Samuha received $40,000.00 each year for two years. This was huge and enabled Samuha to buy a high temperature oven to make leg braces for children with polio as well as several other items of orthotic equipment such as drills, grinders and a bending machine. They also bought a jeep for transporting staff, families and vaccine. They purchased ten sewing machines for older girls with polio for vocational training. They also bought several wheel-chairs, crutches, walkers and shoes. The only stipulation from Rotary was that none of the funds could be used for land or buildings.

At the end of this two year period, Rotary funded my next visit to Samuha so I could monitor how the funds had been used and to make sure that everything was in order. I was able to give a good report back to Rotary and they were amazed that Samuha had used the funds so frugally and wisely. Part of their funding had been to supply a sewing machine for the tailoring program. Samuha managed to buy ten sewing machines for the budgeted amount of one. This donation helped to establish SAMUHA's disability program on a firm footing and SODA as a fund-raising organisation. Around the same time as this, SODA received its charitable status. This was significant for us, as now we could assure all donors that they would receive a tax deductible receipt for their donations, without us having to send the money through Hope International. This encouraged donors to increase their donations.

Once we received charitable status, the SODA Board members changed somewhat as now we needed more extensive book and record keeping. Whereas initially we had all been physios and occupational therapists, now some of them left the group and three nurses joined, one of whom had book-keeping skills and another was experienced at keeping minutes. Around this time, Lesley Schwab, a physiotherapist with a wide network of friends and business acquaintances, joined the group. She was a bundle of energy with a vivacious personality and lots of good ideas.

Lesley suggested that instead of charging admission to our fund-raising dinners, which covered the cost of the dinner and $5.00 extra per plate for the charity, we should make the admission be by donation. The rest of us thought this was very risky but we agreed to try it. By now, our dinners were getting popular enough that instead of booking the Indian restaurant for one night, we now booked it for two consecutive nights. The restaurant could hold sixty guests each night. Lesley's suggestion of admission by donation immediately paid off. People understood that the minimum cost would just cover the meal and everything over that would go to the charity. Some guests paid as much as $500.00 for their dinner instead of the usual $25.00. We always gave a short talk and showed slides of the children we worked with including the progress they were making. This encouraged the guests to dig deep and we started raising much more money at our dinners. Our original goal had been to raise $10,000.00 annually but so far we had never achieved that amount. Now we did.

One year the Sikh Temple in Prince George hosted our dinner. This was tremendously successful as people were most interested to experience the Temple. Also the Sikh community did not charge us for the dinner so all the donations could go directly to Samuha. Incidentally Sikhs comprise two percent of the population of Canada. They also comprise two percent of the population in India.

Another time, we had a silent auction as well as the dinner and this event was extremely successful as a fund-raiser. We held it in the local museum together with some wine-tasting. It was a high-end event which people dressed up for. The grand prize was a diamond ring from a local jeweller and this event was talked about for many years to come. People came to look forward to our annual dinners as being a fun social evening as well as supporting a good cause. We gradually progressed to taking over the Indian restaurant for three consecutive nights and filling it each night and soon we exceeded our $10,000.00 annual fund-raising goal.

19
EVOLUTION OF SAMARTHYA AND A VISIT TO BIHAR.

"Live Simply So Others May Simply Live"

Mahatma Gandhi

In early 2001 Lesley and I returned to Samuha. The train from Bangalore was a big adventure for Lesley. After we had settled down for the night, loud snoring from one of the passengers caused Lesley to sit up and call out, "Who let the dogs out?!"

Everyone else carried on sleeping but the snoring may have diminished a little. Stepping over sleeping bodies at the station on arrival in Raichur was another new experience. We stopped in at the new orthotic workshop in Raichur and were happy to find Siddappa working there. He had undergone training with Ashok and was now helping to make braces for other children with polio. It was wonderful to see his progress from crawling around the village to rehabilitation and school education and now employment with Samuha in the workshop. Without Samuha's interventions, he could have been destined to a life of begging on the streets.

This was Lesley's first trip to see the program. We visited all the different locations of the program including Jalahalli and Koppal but also Haliyal, which was a new area closer to the west coast where Samuha had expanded the program to work with indigenous communities in the area. I also met Dr Kulkarni, who was head of Rotary in Koppal, and since then we have met on every visit to establish a close relationship between Rotary and Samuha as well as SODA.

We made many home visits in the villages. This intrigued Lesley as she absorbed the colourful rural village life. As we walked through the villages, throngs of children excitedly followed us and Lesley captured them all on video, much to their excitement. Hampanna, who was now running the disability program, invited us to his home for dinner and we enjoyed meeting his wife and daughters. We had an elaborate home cooked meal of various flat breads, curried vegetables, fresh fruit and other delicacies. Lesley still communicates with Shobha, their younger daughter.

We also visited Narayanswamy and Chitra's home in Gangavathi and met Kaustubha their young daughter. Again we had a wonderful meal and enjoyed great camaraderie with the family. It was good to see Narayanswamy happily married and obviously thrilled with their young daughter.

As we drove from village to village, we always saw interesting sights. At one home, the grand-parents wove baskets from cane as well as made brooms from a type of palm. Most people worked out in the fields and as we drove to the villages, it was necessary to dodge herds of goats, sheep, buffalo, cattle and numerous dogs and chickens. We also saw monkeys swinging amongst the trees.

Piles of red chillies were spread out drying in the sun. These were then taken to a chilli mill, which could be heard working down the street, and turned into chilli powder. Some villages housed a flour mill, different machines for different grains such as for making rice flour and for millet, which is used for making the staple roti flat bread. Many homes had an indentation on the stone patio in front of the hut where women ground the grain with a large post. It was also common to see two women sitting opposite each other rocking a large rock back and forth to grind tamarind. There is much industry and very little idleness in these rural villages.

After a couple of weeks, Lesley returned to Canada. I spent a couple more weeks with Samuha and participated in the Pulse Polio program. I also did some more training with the team. After a month with Samuha, I flew to Delhi, where I had arranged to meet Cindy, another physiotherapist from Prince George. We had been in touch with the Root Institute in Bodhgaya and had agreed to spend a couple of weeks there helping them with their community based rehabilitation program.

I met Cindy in Delhi where we took a cycle-rickshaw round Old Delhi and visited the Red Fort and Mosque. The Red Fort is an impressive fortification built of red sandstone in the 17th century. It was the main residence of the Mughal Empire and is a UNESCO Heritage site, situated in New Delhi. At the other end of the oldest street in Delhi is the largest mosque in India, Jama Masjid, also built of red sandstone and marble and situated in Old Delhi.

We spent the night in Delhi then took the train from there to Varanassi. We stayed in an old rambling hotel in Varanassi. We wandered around the old city and saw the ghats where funeral pyres send the Hindu spirits on their way. There is a strong sense of history and ritual in the air. We took a boat tour on the Ganges and witnessed many candles floating down the river in respect for those who had died and been burnt on the pyres. Many people were submerging themselves in the holy river and several funeral pyres adorned the ghats. Varanassi is considered by Hindus to be the most holy city in India.

After this interlude, we took another cycle rickshaw back to our hotel for supper and a night's sleep. We booked a private car to take us from Varanassi to Bodhgaya the next morning. This is considered a dangerous route in the poorest state of India, Bihar. We had a good journey and along the road, we saw many camels, loaded with goods. Vehicles are advised to travel in convoys as there is said to be much banditry in the area but we never witnessed any problems.

It took us about six hours by car to reach the Root Institute in Bodhgaya. This Institute is a Buddhist Meditation Centre and a peaceful calm pervaded the senses as soon as we entered the gates. It provides accommodation, meals and training for international followers of Buddhism and meditation. The Institute ran a community based rehabilitation centre run by Dr Sanjay using mostly homeopathic medicine and massage. There were a couple of visiting physiotherapists there. Our role was to assess the children with polio and advise the team on appropriate therapy. We bought some plaster and taught them how to correct deformities with stretching exercises and maintain the correction with plaster casts. There was a nearby orthotic workshop where splints and braces could be made, once the deformities had been corrected.

The Institute provided very comfortable accommodation. There were many Westerners there at the Meditation Centre so the food was more European. It was like a peaceful oasis surrounded by bustling India outside the confines of the campus. There were Tibetan and Bhutanese Temples in the area. Bodhgaya is famous for being where the Buddha attained his enlightenment while sitting under the Bodhi Tree. There is a large Buddhist Temple, which H.H. the Dalai Lama visits annually.

Each day we attended busy polio clinics, sometimes seeing as many as twenty children in a day. It was interesting to see how another program operated and we were glad to have the opportunity to work in this different environment and to provide some advice and recommendations on how best to help the children with polio. We also provided them with Samuha training manuals and made contacts for further follow up with Samuha, as needed. In fact one of the physiotherapists later came to Samuha and spent some time observing how Samuha's disability program worked.

After spending a couple of weeks here, Dr Sanjay drove us to Gaya, where we spent the night in a very run-down hotel. It was so filthy, I didn't dare lie down and fully expected to wind up with bed bugs. The next day we took the train to Delhi, which took eighteen hours. We were constantly offered various types of aromatic food by vendors on the train or through the window at the stations. We secured our luggage under the seat with a chain and padlock. Trains in India always run full. Although they are not fast, they efficiently move thousands of Indians around the country. There are three classes. Third class doesn't have berths and are the most crowded coaches. We always travel in second class, where there are seventy-two berths in each coach, separated into compartments of eight with a corridor running though. First class is air-conditioned and each compartment of six is self-contained, secured with a door, with the corridor running outside the door.

On arrival in Delhi, we took an auto across town to our hotel. The air pollution was intense from all the fumes and traffic. This time we had comfortable and clean accommodation. The next day we spent shopping in various markets to purchase items to sell in Canada for fund-raising for Samuha. The markets teemed with people with insistent merchants selling their wares. I bought some colourful wall-hangings, several pairs of silver anklets and several cotton table cloths and a silk dress for myself. That night I packed up and left by late-night plane to Heathrow for a week in England before continuing on home to Canada. Cindy was on her way to Saudi Arabia.

I had retired from the Prince George Hospital in 2001 and after that did paediatric locums at the local Child

Development Centre and also worked as an itinerant paediatric therapist in several rural communities. I found my experience in India and this work in Canada complemented each other and I was able to transfer skills learnt in each location to my work elsewhere. I continued with this pattern for many years, always saving a two month time-span for travelling to India to work with Samuha with a stop-off in England to visit family. Floyd managed at home and I'm sure enjoyed his freedom.

Samuha's disability program continued to expand. Samuha built a new campus at Irkalgada, a site we had visited earlier and found suitable. The following year, when I returned with students, this is where we stayed. Samuha established a tailoring centre there as a vocational training centre for older girls, who were disabled from polio. The girls stayed on campus for the six month course and then were provided with a sewing machine to take back to their village so they could establish their business and support themselves financially.

A couple of years later, Camille, an occupational therapy student came with me to Samuha. One of the projects we did was to make air cushions to fit in wheel-chairs for clients with spinal cord injury. SODA had bought an expensive Roho cushion for Shankar, an accountant who had joined the staff of Samuha. He had previously been involved in an accident and suffered a spinal cord injury. As usual in India, he had been discharged home without any advice on follow up for further care or therapy. He didn't know the importance of relieving pressure regularly on his buttocks, as he had no sensation there so couldn't feel any pain. He developed severe pressure sores and wound up having to have high level amputations of both of his legs. Samuha employed him as an accountant but he needed to be able to sit to perform this task so he needed a special cushion. SODA was happy to supply this for Shankar but we couldn't afford to keep doing this for other clients as the cushions are so expensive and we wouldn't have enough funds to assist the rest of the program.

The book, Disabled Village Children written by David Werner, had detailed instructions on how to make pressure relieving cushions so we took on this challenge. We used inner tubes from bicycle tyres. We filled them with air then folded them longitudinally and joined them together to fit the size of the wheelchair seat. We had to make sure that no valves or other rough parts could be in the weight-bearing surface to cause a problem on the clients skin. This was a fairly laborious task but certainly drastically reduced the cost of the cushions. All we had to do was buy the tubes and the rest was volunteer labour. These cushions served us for a while but now there is a much superior cost-effective model available locally in Tamil Nadu.

On one of our free evenings at Irkalgada campus, a group of us climbed up the rocky outcropping, where we had visited a couple of years previously. This was just a short walk from the campus then a climb up a jumble of large steep rocks. From the top we were able to watch the sun set in the west at the same time as the moon rose in the east, it was truly spectacular. The vantage point also gave us a good view of all the surrounding agriculture and scattered villages. The sky is unique in India as without light pollution from electric light, we were dazzled each night by all the stars. The moon looks as though it's lying on its back compared to the view from Canada. One night we noticed two stars above the crescent of the moon and one of the disability workers quietly said, 'Look, there's a happy face!" That is truly what it looked like, a giant happy face in the sky.

All the staff are very aware of the night sky and Black Moon Day, each month, is considered special. Due to lack of light pollution, it is wonderful to see all the constellations and the milky way, which are often hidden from us in Canada. Babumiya invited us to his home on Black Moon Day for a meal of lamb curry and special sweets. He continued to make strides in his recovery from his spinal cord injury. He was now in charge of the disability program in Deodurg and was able to drive a motor-bike again. He still had a marked limp and some difficulty with his hand function but he was doing remarkably well.

Samuha's disability program by this time had coined the name Samarthya, which means 'ability' in Sanskrit. The full name is now called Samuha Samarthya. This program has continued to grow and thrive and SODA has also continued to grow and now we always reached our $10,000.00 target annually to send to Samuha. As these funds increased, we were able to expand the reach and effectiveness of Samarthya, always working towards their identified goals.

20
KANAKAGIRI AND WORLD DISABILITY DAY:

"My disability is that I cannot use my legs. My handicap is your negative perception of that disability and thus of me" Rick Hansen (Man in Motion)

In 2004, I returned to Samuha with two more students from UBC. This time we stayed at the new campus at Kanakagiri. Samuha had now made this campus their headquarters, where the main administration took place and the health and education programs ran from here. Samarthya was just initiating a horticultural vocational training program for young men with disability.

A simple walk from the Samuha campus, to the town could be an adventure in itself. Once outside the gates, we followed a dirt track flanked on each side by green hedgerows. Boys on bicycles, women carrying their supplies on their heads, a small boy with a few goats, a man leading some oxen and another man sitting atop his slow plodding bullock cart could all be encountered at a leisurely pace. When Samuha first moved there, some of the villagers greeted us with incredulous stares, others with a friendly, "Hi, what is your name?" All were barefoot with no flesh to spare on their bony limbs. As we returned annually to this campus, the local villagers got used to us and accepted our oddity. It can feel intimidating to be observed as a visible minority.

As we reached the town, excited children came running out wanting to shake our hands and groups of them accompanied us on our way. We found small shops selling vegetables, hard-ware, clothes, silver jewellery, cell phones, rope and more. Some young boys decided to be our guides and took us across fields to see ancient temples and old sunken rectangular bathing places surrounded by rows of steps leading down into the water. These were historic relics from an ancient kingdom.

After these diversions and having received directions on how to return to campus, we accepted a ride from a bullock cart driver, as we had strayed several kilometers from our route. We climbed up and sat on the wooden boards amongst the family members, much to the amusement of passers-by. One man even stopped his motor bike to take our photo, a reversal of the usual roles. It turned out that he was a local newspaper reporter and the following day the staff excitedly showed us that we were featured in the local paper.

The main purpose of the walk, apart from exercise, was to buy bananas and find an international phone. but international phones were not available. By the time we returned to campus, two hours later, the bananas had been shared with the occupants of the bullock cart so we returned empty handed but enriched by our little adventure.

It turns out that our walk into the town, although eventful, was a much safer means of transportation than our usual motor-cycle ride to the villages. One of the

Canadian students met with an accident as the result of a burst rear tire and she and her driver both needed attention at the local hospital to treat their severe road rash, after being thrown from the bike and dragged down the road. Fortunately there were no broken bones and both were able to resume their work after a few days. Driving is a hair-raising experience at the best of times as the rule seems to be that the biggest vehicle wins. This often is not decided until the last second when one has to swerve on to the shoulder to avoid collision with oncoming buses or trucks.

One day the Samuha campus was full of women, some of whom were traditional birth attendants and others who were village health workers from the surrounding villages. They were participating in a training camp organized by the Samuha health team and were learning about herbal medicine and nutrition. When I first spent time with Samuha, the Traditional Birth Attendants were using dung to heal the umbilical cord and the knives used for cutting the cord, were often not clean. Post-partum tetanus at that time was not uncommon and was a cause of neo-natal deaths. Hygiene is much improved now.

Shortly after this health training camp, the disability program initiated the horticultural training program for people with disability. This entailed a one year residential course teaching techniques of dry land horticulture, soil enrichment and vermi-composting, seed collection and propagation as well as the nutritional values of the different plants and herbs. Vitamin and micro-nutrient deficiencies were common in the villages and contributed to disease and disability such as visual impairment from vitamin A deficiency, and rickets from vitamin D deficiency.

Even diabetes was on the increase, possibly the result of increased white rice in the diet as opposed to the whole grain flat breads, which are more traditional and nutritious. Also with more mechanisation and education, some villagers were turning away from manual labour and labour intensive agriculture to a more sedentary lifestyle. This gradual decrease in physical activity.is probably a contributing factor to the increase in the incidence of diabetes.

On one of our visits to a home in Kanakagiri, we met a young boy, named Durugappa, who was lying in bed and unable to move. The family had spent many rupees taking him all over India to various Temples and Doctors, looking for a cure. He had become progressively weaker, despite their best efforts. When we examined him, I found that he could move his limbs a little but he didn’t have enough strength to roll over in bed independently. His sensation was intact and he was able to speak clearly. The team all thought he had polio but the history told us otherwise.

Polio comes on with a fever and weakness over a few days but in this case, he had become progressively weaker over several weeks. The fact that he had normal sensation showed that his brain and spinal cord weren’t affected. I thought he most likely had Guillaine Barre syndrome, which is a lower motor neurone disease often preceded by a mild illness. The progression of weakness can continue until the respiratory muscles are also affected and, without intervention, the patient could die from respiratory distress. Where adequate medical facilities exist, the treatment would be replacement of plasma, or plasmapheresis. This usually results in full recovery but sometimes the client is left with residual weakness.

At this visit we helped Durugappa sit up on the edge of the bed. He needed support to maintain this position. We showed the family some simple leg exercises they could do with Durugappa to help him regain some muscle strength. We promised the family we would come back frequently to gradually progress these exercises. Fortunately they lived close to the campus in Kanakagiri. We returned a few days later and were happy to find that Durugappa could now turn himself in bed. He still needed help to get from lying to sitting but he could now maintain that position with the support of his arms. He was able to move his legs while sitting. These were all signs of gradual progress.

A week later, we found him already sitting up and he could now straighten his legs, while sitting. Two of us decided to help him to stand. He was able to maintain this position, with our support for a few minutes. We showed the family how to help him to move from lying to sitting to standing and asked them to gradually extend the time Durgappa could stand and if possible, gradually reduce the amount of support they gave him. They were very happy with this progress. We also explained to the family how they could build a set of parallel bars outside their home for Durugappa to practice standing and hopefully walking.

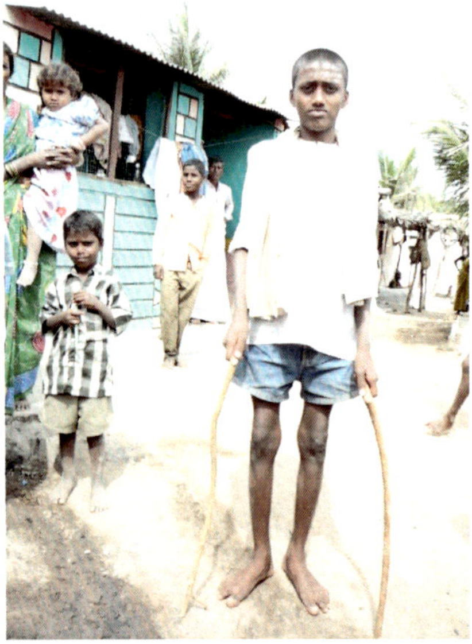

Durgappa outside his home

By the end of our six weeks at Kanakagiri, Durugappa was able to walk on flat ground with the help of two sticks, which his father had made for him. Durugappa was beaming at this progress and his family were so thankful that we were able to help him and without any cost. They thought we had wrought miracles. In fact Durugappa may have recovered spontaneously but he was certainly helped by an effective physiotherapy program.

The horticulture program plans came to fruition. Samuha hired two trainers, one who had experience in plant propagation and seed collection and another who had a background in nutrition and herbal remedies. Six young men were selected to be the first clients, most of them had been affected by polio and one of them was in a wheel-chair due to his inability to walk. Apart from learning the horticulture skills, their continued rehabilitation was also taken care of by teaching strengthening exercises and by fitting and upgrading their splints and braces.

An area of land had been set aside for this program. They built raised beds for more efficient watering and planting. Several trees were planted for both shade and food production. A herbal garden was designed in squares for each herb variety and slightly sloped to take full advantage of the sun. They built a greenhouse so they could start off many of the plants indoors. This area became a beautiful, peaceful location once the fruit trees became established and medicinal herbs and other vegetables and floral plants were grown.

A vermi-composting system was set up. They even purchased a buffalo so the clients could learn how to look after it and to milk it, then the milk was used for the campus staff. Eventually the team were taught marketing skills and took their produce to the local market, once it was harvested. The plan was that once these horticulture students had finished their program, they could return to their villages and grow nutritional food to sell in the market. They could also find work in larger nurseries.

Talking about buffalo, we heard an interesting story on one of our visits in the village. We were working with a child with paralysed legs, from a birth defect. We had made him some braces and his parents had built a set of parallel bars outside for him to practice walking, which he tried during this visit. Afterwards we went back inside the house for tea and while sitting on the floor chatting with the family, I noticed the buffalo tied up just below us with a small calf standing nearby. The family seeing my gaze related this story: A month previously the buffalo had given birth to a calf which only survived two weeks. When the calf died, the buffalo stopped producing milk. The family relied on this animal for their milk so they skinned the dead calf and stuffed the hide with straw and stood it next to the buffalo. It looked very realistic and we saw the buffalo lick and nuzzle this fake calf a few times. The plan worked and the family got their daily ration of milk and the buffalo seemed content!

A sports day and cultural program was held to celebrate World Disability Day on December 3rd each year. Although there had been no new cases of polio there for the last few years, there were still many with residual paralysis from this disease. It was inspiring to see so many with seriously deformed limbs, compete in these events. The races were categorized for one crutch, two crutches, one leg-brace, two braces, mildly affected requiring no aids, severely affected with no aids (crawling) and tricycle races. There were also athletic events for people who had visual impairments, speech &

hearing impairments and for people with intellectual disability.

It is amazing how fast some of these people, whose hips and knees are permanently deformed, can move by propelling themselves with their hands. One man hopped the whole 100 metre course, and won his event. People with amputations and those with leprosy or polio all competed against each other and had fun in the process. The event took place in an open field under the unrelenting sun.

The sports were followed by a communal lunch and evening cultural program. Several schools for children with disabilities participated with songs, dance and drama. Competitors beamed as they received their prizes including Balavva, the young girl who I first met in her village, fourteen years earlier. At that time, she was dragged through the streets by her brothers, on a makeshift wooden cart, in order to get to school. Her hips and knees were fixed in a bent position. Samuha arranged for her to have corrective surgery then made braces for her legs and provided crutches. In no time, she was walking with a big smile on her face. It was heart-warming to see the determination on her face when she was running with crutches and the big smile when she received her prize. One of the big advantages to me of returning to India on an annual basis was that I could see the progress of these children. Balavva was now in high school and participating fully in village life.

Several members of Samuha staff competed in these sports, including Virupakshi Hadpad from Deodurg, who had polio and wears one leg brace with a four inch shoe raise. Also Lakshman, one of the horticulture trainees with polio, who competed and won his heat of the tricycle races. The tricycles are hand propelled and made with three bicycle wheels with a bench seat. They are largely used by adults with a disability instead of wheel-chairs as they are much faster and handle the rough roads better than a wheel-chair.

There was one man with very short legs. He had normal feet but it looked as though his feet were attached directly below his thighs. He could walk but used a three - wheeled scooter for faster mobility. A local politician, who had bilateral amputations without prostheses, seemed to be the main organizer of the program. He needed to be lifted from the ground on to a chair and used a tricycle for mobility.

Events such as these help to raise the standing of people with disability in the community. They are accepted by many but still there is stigma amongst the uneducated that disability is caused as punishment from an earlier life. Sometimes Samuha has to intervene when people are turned down for government jobs or training programs, when they qualify academically but are denied due to their disability. These appeals are usually successful. Fortunately the polio epidemic was drawing to a close.

21
CRITTERS, TERRORISM & FLOODS;

"Be truthful, gentle and fearless:" Mahatma Gandhi

We continue to return to Samuha annually with Canadian physio and occupational therapy students, mostly from UBC but also from Queens. We have expanded to taking four students each time, preferably two occupational therapy and two physio students so they can learn from each other and learn the essentials of integrated health care. Samuha also needs both disciplines to help their clients. Samuha now has four different disability sites; the two campuses at Irkalgada and at Kanakagiri and the two programs in the towns of Koppal and Deodurg. We were accommodated at Kanakagiri for many years, which was a delightfully tree-shaded campus and included the horticulture program.

My hut in Kanakagiri was close to the kitchen. There was a wooden door on the hut but the windows just had vertical bars but no glass. The roof extended beyond the mud walls but there was a gap between the roof and walls for ventilation. One day the kitchen staff heard a scream coming from my room. A rat ran across my keyboard while I was writing on the computer! The staff thought this was extremely funny. They, the rats, often ran in and out of my hut. When I was reading the newspaper in the office, a rat often scurried around the room. One night there were eight rats in the women's dorm but some of those were then annihilated, probably the result of the loud thudding which we heard that morning.

One year there was actually an outbreak of Plague, which was quite alarming. There were signs at all the train stations advising people to take precautions against the plague. Occasionally you would see people wearing masks, whether they had the plague, I never asked. None of the Samuha staff seemed to be at all concerned.

A frog accompanied the students in their shower room and lizards, or geckos, frequented the walls of most of the rooms and could be heard chirping in the evening. There was a large array of insects, including zillions of tiny ants, large orange and white striped spiders, big noisy flying beetles - the size of cockroaches as well as the usual wasps, bees and mosquitoes. The security of a mosquito net did wonders to afford a peaceful night's rest without having to worry about any of these intruders.

On one visit to Jalahalli, as I was being shown to my hut, one of the staff said, “There was a cobra under your bed yesterday. We had to remove it.”
My eyebrows raised as I thought to myself, “I think I'd rather not have known that.”

They were doing construction and clearing out the ditches along the road so that had probably disturbed the snake. To access the bathroom, I had to walk down an unlit path bordered by vegetation. Also the door to my hut had about a two inch gap underneath it. One thing I've learnt from my travels to India is to not worry about things – what will happen, will happen. More recently we saw a cobra outside the wall of the kitchen in Koppal. On a village visit to Karigudda with Narayanswamy we saw a skinny white snake emerging from the top of a rock pile. We took a wide detour from that path so I imagine it must have been quite venomous.

One day we were sitting around the Mess at Kanakagiri having breakfast when I heard the breaking news of the Mumbai terrorist attacks in 2008. I was listening to the ten minute English radio news offered daily at breakfast time. I informed the others sitting around the kitchen area and they showed a moment of concern and then continued their current conversations saying, "That's a long way away from here." Mumbai might as well be in England or America. For many, there is no concept of what the rest of the world is like outside these clusters of villages. It feels disconcerting to be in a foreign country when terrorism strikes, particularly when it is targeted towards foreign tourists. Mumbai/Bombay is however seven hundred kilometres from Koppal but it is the capital of the neighbouring state. The places targeted were mostly five star hotels, whereas our hotel in Bangalore has no stars.

It wasn't until the next day, when the English cricket team decided to withdraw and fly back to England, that there was any interest, cricket being the national sport in India. There was even more consternation when India cancelled their proposed series with Pakistan. The causes of this terrorism event were not clear but the most rational argument was that Al Quaeda co-ordinated the event, as evidenced by the British, American and Israeli targets, using India as a location due to its lax security. Organisations of Indian Muslims, frustrated by Hindu Fundamentalist factions, helped by providing local knowledge, hideouts and language skills.

India has been a thriving democracy since the demise of the British Empire in India followed by Partition, when it gained Independence in 1947. Partition was a violent event with lots of bloodshed when the Indian subcontinent was divided into majority Hindu India and Muslim Pakistan. Pakistan later further split when Bangaladesh was formed. Kashmir is still disputed territory between India and Pakistan. Ever since independence, India has strived to be an inclusive secular democracy building tolerance of religion and race. In recent years this inclusiveness has shown signs of weakening since the weakening of power of the Congress Party. The BJP, a Hindu Fundamentalist Party has fascist elements bent on causing disunity. Presently there is a coalition government in place but the BJP is still able to exert its influence. India is predominantly Hindu, approximately seventy five percent and twenty percent Muslim with a few Christians, Buddhist and other religions. India needs to come together to protect this largest of all democracies. It is important to build tolerance and not engage in fear mongering.

Shortly after the Mumbai incident, Samuha received special funding for a new building in Koppal. This is situated two kilometres outside the town and houses the orthotic workshop, the administration offices, training hall, accommodation for staff and visitors and kitchen and eating area. It is close to a busy highway on a bus route, so is convenient for clients, and is surrounded on three sides by fields. Samuha developed a kitchen garden with several shade trees as well as avocados and papaya. Once this centre was established, we started staying there on our visits, instead of at Kanakagiri.

In 2010 there were severe floods particularly in the Deodurg area. The Canadian contingent arrived shortly after this event. In October, after a drought had been declared, it started raining and didn't stop for four days. The mud huts couldn't withstand the torrential rain and many of them collapsed. Fortunately the villagers anticipated that they may lose their homes so most of them moved to safer locations in time to avoid being crushed. There were a few deaths but not as many as there would have been had it been a more sudden event.

Soon after our arrival we visited some of these flood affected villages. Apart from the direct rain damage, several rivers broke their banks and flooded the area. We visited one such village, where the river flowed right through their homes. Most of the livestock were carried away in the flood and drowned. The grain, which was stored in pits, was also destroyed. The villagers had watched the river steadily rise and hoped that it would recede before reaching their homes but once it was obvious that they were in danger, the whole village started walking to safety. They walked seventeen kilometres through the night in the rain to the nearest town. Some old people and young children had to be carried the distance. One villager, who was 103 years old, reported that he had never seen anything like it before in his long life.

The Government offered compensation of $175.00 to villagers who had lost their homes from rain damage but there was no compensation for those affected by the river damage. Of course this amount didn't begin to pay for the cost of rebuilding their homes but it was hoped it would see them through the short term of finding enough food to sustain the families. The Government later moved this village to higher ground, away from the river, but the villagers still had to pay for their home construction.

One older lady was sitting in despair in the middle of the rubble, which used to be her home. It is tragic to see these people, who are already impoverished, having lost everything they possessed. She probably only owned the sari she was wearing and nothing else. Family members will always support each other but it looked as though this lady was all alone.

Samuha supported families with disability who lost their homes but the task was overwhelming. There were 145 such families. Whole areas were cut off due to collapsed road and rail bridges. There was also no phone or electricity connection. It took a month for the major rail and road routes to be re-opened.

Three of the disability workers lost their homes and their crops. Many farmers lost their equipment. One girl with polio, who had just completed Samuha's tailoring program and had set up her shop with sewing machine, lost the building and contents in the flood. India did not ask for or receive any international assistance for this disaster but many families still suffer from their losses. S.O.D.A. helped with funds to support families with disability to rebuild their homes.

Having visited the flood ravaged areas around Deodurg, we returned to Koppal. It had also suffered floods and some bridges were washed out but it was not nearly as severe as in Deodurg.

Prior to the floods, we always saw various local crafts and cottage industries as we travelled from village to village such as people making bricks from the bright red soil, which is moulded then baked in small brick ovens. We often saw others making rope from sisal plants, which lined the road. The coarse fibres were stripped from the leaves then twined into bundles. These bundles were picked up by brightly coloured trucks and taken to a shed, where others plied the fibres into various thicknesses of rope, using simple machines.

When the fields of sunflowers ripened they were harvested, mostly for their oil. Castor oil and linseed oil were also grown locally. Large groves of papaya used to be seen ripening and coconuts and bananas were always plentiful as were fresh onions and tomatoes and many other vegetables.

All of these harvesting and other activities were halted in the flood affected villages as their crops and equipment were destroyed. It took them several years to recover because their stored crop from the previous year was destroyed as well as their new crop and now they had mostly lost their equipment and many of their animals too. These are the tragedies and hardships of life in rural India.

22
END OF POLIO & EVOLUTION OF NEW PROGRAMS:

"It matters if you just don't give up" Stephen Hawking

Thanks to the efforts of the World Health Organisation, (WHO), and Rotary International, polio was eradicated in India in 2011. In Samuha's villages, we didn't see any more new cases of polio after 2004. India still continues with the Pulse Polio program, which vaccinates every child under five twice each year. This will continue until polio is eradicated in Pakistan and Afghanistan to make sure that the polio virus cannot again infect its citizens. Presently families coming into India from Pakistan must vaccinate their children under five at the border. If they refuse, they are not allowed entry.

Some countries believe that the polio vaccine is a western plot to sterilize their citizens. As long as this level of mistrust exists, India must continue to vaccinate all their children. During the height of this epidemic, every child under two was infected by the virus. Paralysis occurs in only 1percent of those infected but the results of this were catastrophic. There is so much disability in India, largely attributed to polio. This disease is entirely preventable through vaccination.

Since there is such a high level of illiteracy in India and many rural people rely on agriculture, it is extremely tough for people affected by polio to gain useful employment. Non-Government Organisations, NGOs, like Samuha have provided many opportunities for rehabilitation, income generation and vocational training but there are so many areas of India which do not have access to such organisations so people are condemned to a life of hardship on the streets. Since the eradication of polio in Samuha's villages, we have expanded the program to work with children with all kinds of disabilities. We now also work with adults, many of whom have spinal cord injury.

SODA's original goal was to raise $10,000.00 annually but we later had a couple of specific fund-raising objectives. The first was to build and staff an Early Intervention Centre in Koppal to provide rehabilitation services to children with disability under six years of age, to prepare them for school.

Our fund-raising dinners in Prince George had become so popular that we now booked the Indian restaurant for three consecutive nights. We always sold out with a capacity of sixty supporters per night. We showed slides of the work we were doing with Samuha and when people saw all the children with disability who needed help, they were only too pleased to raise their donations and support the program. The talk and slide show never failed to bring tears to Floyd's eyes and his pride in our work was obvious.

We were able to raise enough funds to build and equip this Early Intervention Centre and it has been full to capacity ever since. Prabhakar was hired to lead and develop this program. He has a wonderful way with children and their families and the Centre has gained an excellent reputation in Koppal District. It is housed in the Koppal building and is situated opposite the orthotic workshop.

We chose the equipment needed by modelling it on the Child Development Centre in Prince George. We discussed the needs with the team and they found people locally who could make the equipment. This included large two inch thick mats to cover the floor and wedge cushions and high density foam filled rolls to use for exercise and support as well as a set of foam steps, which the children could climb on and learn to crawl. They installed mirrors down one wall so the children could find stimulation. There is a set of wall bars and a local artist painted beautiful Indian scenes on the walls. We bought stimulating and educational toys to help the children with hand dexterity and co-ordination.

This Centre became the Canadian students' main focus for the next few years, both for the students to gain paediatric skills and for us to support Prabhakar and his team in developing this important program. The orthotic technician also needed to learn new skills to make special seats for these children and to make foot orthotics to help them to walk. The Centre continues to grow and provides a much needed service.

Samuha designed a similar space in Deodurg and the paediatric equipment was shared between the two areas. Babumiya has developed the centre in Deodurg, which is well respected in the community with many referrals coming from the local paediatrician. Babumiya is training a junior disability worker to help him as well as an orthotic technician. A speech and hearing program, with a separate team of workers, also runs from this centre, headed by Virupakshi Hadpad.

The teams in each centre also continue to provide services in the villages through home visits. On one such visit we met Kaveri, who was a six year old girl with spina bifida. This is a congenital condition where the spinal cord protrudes through the spinal column and causes paralysis and lack of sensation below the level of the protrusion. Kaveri had weakness of both legs and loss of sensation in her left lower leg. Due to this lack of sensation, she developed a deep wound on her left heel. This should have been prevented through diligent medical care but sadly she had to undergo a below knee amputation. She had good control of her hips and knees but her right ankle was very weak. On our visit, we determined that she needed a splint for the right ankle and a prosthesis for the left leg. We taught Kaveri hip and leg strengthening exercises and encouraged the family to build a set of parallel bars outside their home so Kaveri could practice walking on her one leg.

Kaveri

On our next visit, the bars had been built and Kaveri was diligent with her exercises. The family also helped her get to school so she wouldn't miss out on her education. They agreed to bring Kaveri to the orthotic workshop for fitting of a prosthesis, which they did the following week. It would take some practice for Kaveri to get used to this new leg but then we hoped she would be able to walk to school independently. This visit was a great learning experience for the Canadian students and an exciting moment for Kaveri.

The travelling from village to village was one of the main highlights of the Canadian students' trips. They saw huge mounds of hay carried on wooden carts pulled by pairs of oxen, with their gaily painted horns. Pairs of brown skinny legs could be seen under large piles of hay, as young boys walked down the road carrying the loads on their heads. Colourfully dressed women washed their clothes by beating them against the rocks as they sat along the banks of canals and rivers or any other available body of water, while partially submerged buffalo were washed by their handlers enjoying the cool but murky water.

To begin with I thought our jeep driver was inconsiderate when he drove over bundles of millet strewn across the road but it turns out this is the accepted way of thrashing the grain. The grain is then swept up and placed in metal trays and scattered from a height on to a sheet so the chaff blows away and the grain drops on to the sheet and is bagged for storage.

On one village trip, we saw three men working in a forge inside someone's hut, making horse shoes and shaping other metal equipment. This operation consisted of a central fire over which one man held a piece of iron resting on a grate. Another man repeatedly hit the red hot iron with a sledge-hammer. Meantime the third man worked a bellows on a long rope to keep the fire burning hot enough to forge the metal.

It was common to see men and women wielding sledge-hammers as they transformed piles of large rocks, dumped alongside the road, into piles of coarse gravel for road repair. This back-breaking task was done barefoot and with no eye protection.

We always traveled to the accompaniment of a cacophony of horns as jeeps tried to pass loaded trucks, bullock carts and herds of sheep without dropping off the narrow pavement on to the soft shoulder. We met loaded buses with several passengers sitting on top and jeeps with people clinging to the sides, front, back and roof. Motorbikes carried whole families and bicycles often carried at least two, completing the colours, sights and sounds of rural India.

After establishing the Early Intervention Centre, the next project was to build a spinal cord injury unit. I had found that adults with spinal cord injury were not surviving beyond two years from their injury. They were being discharged home from hospital without any advice or therapy.

In rural India, people sleep on the ground with just a thin straw mat for bedding. People with spinal cord injury have no sensation below the level of their injury. They should be turned every two hours to relieve the pressure on their skin and that is on a western mattress. Because they can't feel pain and can't turn themselves, they often develop severe pressure sores. If these are not treated and the pressure is not relieved then they go on to develop septicaemia, which is a common cause of death for these clients. Another problem is urinary tract infections. Because they lose their bowel and bladder control, they are at high risk for developing infections. This also can lead to death.

Once we realised this problem, we decided we needed to build a spinal cord injury unit. The plan was that this should be a transitional care facility to offer rehabilitation after the client leaves acute care in the hospital and prior to returning home to their village. We could then educate the clients and their families on how to manage their lives and prevent further injury. We fund-raised through a "buy a brick" campaign in Prince George where donors could buy a brick for $25.00. We started this in November and by January, we had raised enough money to build this unit. Samuha decided to house this unit at Irkalgada, where some buildings already existed. The area was beautifully treed and close to the highway. That year, we sent $35,000. to Samuha to run the program and to build the Spinal Cord Injury unit. Ever since this major fund-raising effort, SODA's goal increased to sending $20,000.00 annually and we have recently always exceeded this amount.

The next campaign was to raise enough money for the exercise equipment required to rehabilitate these clients. Again it only took a few months to realise our goal as donors knew their money was going directly to help these clients rebuild their lives.

On our next visit to India, it was the occupational therapy student's goal to design this unit so it would be accessible for clients in wheel-chairs. It was the physiotherapy student's goal to determine the exercise equipment needed to strengthen the upper body so these clients would be able to transfer themselves easily as well as manage crutches, if they were able. We designed the unit to ensure that the clients could be independent in toileting. The accommodation was built so that clients could transfer themselves from their wheel-chair to their beds and they could also navigate the kitchen and prepare their meals.

The whole campus was ramped so they could independently wheel themselves from one building to another. The plan was that the clients could stay there up to three months to learn the necessary skills to prepare themselves for the village. We also developed some vocational training so they could learn tailoring and horticultural skills to help with some income generation. Family members could come and stay for the first few days to enable the clients to settle in and to understand the goals of the program but after that the clients needed to learn independence.

We equipped the physiotherapy gym with springs and pulleys, a set of wall bars, parallel bars and a weight machine. The carpenter made high mats, at the same level as the wheel-chairs so the clients could transfer themselves independently. A frame was fitted above these mats to facilitate attachment of slings and springs for resisted exercises to strengthen the upper body.

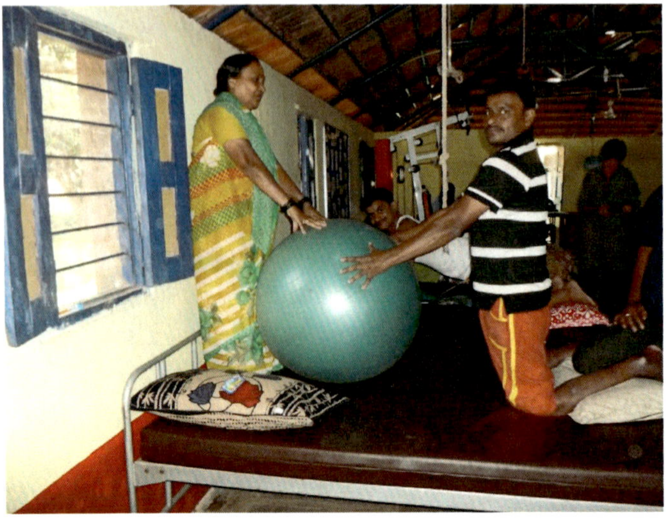

Spinal Cord Injury Unit

Initially we started this program for five clients. It is the only spinal cord injury unit in the area so it has become very popular with referrals coming in even from Bangalore. It became obvious that we would soon need to expand the scope of the program.

Koppal houses the main disability program and is half an hour's drive from the spinal cord injury unit at Irkalgada campus. Koppal has become our main headquarters when the Canadian team of students visit annually, enabling them to share their time between the Early Intervention Centre and the Spinal Cord Injury Unit as well as continue with home visits. The students also spend a few days in Deodurg to help with their smaller Early Intervention Centre and to advise on their spinal cord injured clients. These clients are transferred to the Unit in Irkalgada when more intensive interventions are needed. Samuha's program continues to evolve.

PART 3

TWENTY FOUR YEARS LATER:

23
PROGRESSION OF S.O.D.A. AND SAMUHA SAMARTHYA:

"Don't judge each day by the harvest you reap, but by the seeds you plant" R.L. Stevenson

Samuha Overseas Development Association, (S.O.D.A), continues to develop and expand its role. As of 2016, we have taken a total of thirty five Canadian Physiotherapy and Occupational Therapy students with us to India for their six week practicums towards their Masters degree. One of these students, Hana, graduated as a physiotherapist then went into Medical School to become a paediatrician, having gained her initial paediatric experience as a student with Samuha. Her goal is to become a paediatric physiatrist, which would incorporate both of her disciplines. She happens to be the grand-daughter of the late King of Syria!

Several students continue to support Samuha through ventures such as an annual volleyball tournament in Ontario, marathon running with pledges to Samuha, annual Christmas donations and another supporter in Whitwell, England, makes and sells jam to support Samuha's work.

Andrea Mendoza, who first went to Samuha as a student, decided to become a preceptor herself and has returned to Samuha twice since her student visit. She stayed there for six months in the winter of 2015/16 to help progress the Early Intervention Centre and Spinal Cord Injury Unit and to update the training manuals. She also took several orthotic trainers and students as well as physiotherapy instructors. Andrea expanded our fundraising capabilities through crowd-funding initiatives.

Students: Kailen, Maegan, Marcia. Hilary & Andrea. Danielle

Our circle of supporters continues to expand as word spreads about all the good work that Samuha is doing in India. We have moved our fund-raising dinners to a Banqueting Hall, to accommodate two hundred guests. We combine this with a silent auction and Indian entertainment such as dancing, turban wrapping and henna painting. Lesley's Dad was a good sport and was the first volunteer for the turban wrapping, which he then wore for the rest of the night! We always show slides of the previous year's work and as word passes on, more and more people come out to support our functions. It is an event that is looked forward to annually. We may soon have to hold the function on two consecutive nights or else have both a summer and winter event. When we tell the guests, "Every cent raised goes directly to help families with disability" they are happy to donate and appreciate the hands-on approach of the charity.

Our Board continues to evolve. Elaine, who is a nurse on our Board, came with me for a month on one of our visits. Prior to heading to Samuha, we decided to go to Rajasthan for a couple of weeks. This is the most colourful state in India and quite different from the south. It is in the northwest and borders the Thar desert, which also borders Pakistan. We visited the Temple cities of Jodhpur, Jaipur and Udaipur, spending a night in each city. Udaipur was my favourite with its beautiful marble architecture and narrow cobbled streets. We also visited Jaisalmer on the edge of the desert where camels take visitors for rides deeper towards the border. We arrived in Pushkar the day before their famous camel festival, which is a huge annual event, where they barter camels, horses and cattle. It was already bustling with activity. For anyone visiting India as a tourist, I would strongly recommend a tour of Rajasthan. We hired a private car and driver so we could visit all the sites of interest.

Elaine's role at Samuha was to teach wound care particularly for the spinal cord injured clients and their care-givers. She made a reference book for the team, which they refer to, with simple instructions and diagrams for prevention of pressure sores and healing techniques. They continue to refer to this manual. Elaine also introduced the idea of using honey to promote wound healing. Honey is readily available locally and reasonably priced so this was a cost-effective solution. It is used as a topical wound covering and is kept in place with gauze.

Jeannie, an Occupational Therapy colleague with paediatric experience, came with me one year. Her teaching and advice was invaluable for the team and I am hoping that she may return for some more follow-up in the future. She taught Prabhakar and his assistants some hand dexterity skills for the children as well as feeding techniques and seating advice, all of which have proved most useful. She also taught use of appropriate toys according to the level and ability of the child.

Phil, another Canadian physiotherapist, went to Samuha as a preceptor with four students. After completing that assignment in 2015, he went on to Nepal to volunteer with an organisation there. Shortly after finishing his work he continued to the Annapurna Range in Nepal for some exploration and was there when the massive earthquake hit. He immediately made his way back to Pokhara, Nepal, and stayed there many months to help with rehabilitation of so many injured victims of the quake. He later became chair of the Global Health Division of the Canadian Physiotherapy Association.

Lesley has accompanied me three times to India and continues to invigorate the program with her enthusiasm and commitment. One year Lesley and her mother, Colleen, who was born in Calcutta, both joined me in India. We travelled by train to Mysore for an outing one week-end. This is a beautiful city a few hours' drive west from Bangalore. There we visited the stately Mysore Palace, which dates back to 1912 and is the Royal seat of the Maharajas of Mysore. It is one of the most impressive buildings in India, situated in the centre of the city and built of granite with several pink marble domes.

This palace is famous for its Dussehra Parade of elephants, which celebrates an important Hindu festival. Several elephants are housed at the palace and we noticed some of them in the palace grounds being ridden by their mahouts so we wandered over to see them. The mahouts signalled that we should take their photos, so we did but then the elephants stretched out their trunks for money. We gave a chunk of money to one of them and thought that should be good enough but then the elephants pushed us back against the wall, dwarfing and intimidating us while the mahouts smiled and stretched out their hands. They wouldn't let us go until we gave them some more money to each of them, which was quite un-nerving for several minutes.

The Early Intervention Centre in Koppal continues to expand. Prabhakar, who is in charge of this centre, is now married with two children and the family live in Koppal. Most of the CBR staff are now married with children so live in their own homes in the villages and commute to work daily. As the children grow, education for the children becomes important and families have to carefully consider where their children will go to school and make sure they have access to suitable transportation. Samuha has increased staff remuneration to make sure they have sufficient funds for their growing families.

Through Andrea's help, the Early Intervention Centre in Koppal is much better organised after some renovations. It now has a separate room for early education and another room for family support and counselling with a maximum of three families in the therapy room. This is working well and Prabhakar has trained four more support workers to help with the program. He also provides outreach to community primary care centres and assesses young children to ensure they are reaching their developmental milestones. If not, they can come to the centre for help or Prabhakar will continue to follow them bi-weekly in the primary care centres.

Babumiya also runs the Early Intervention Centre in Deodurg, a four hour drive from Koppal. He has two assistants. Samuha has orthotic workshops in Koppal, Raichur and a small one in Deodurg. Clients with spinal cord injuries in the Deodurg area are seen at home or referred to the spinal cord injury unit in Koppal District in Irkalgada.

The spinal cord injury unit has made huge gains in quality and has expanded to be able to receive fifteen clients instead of the original plan of five. Some clients just come for short stay for assessment and advice but most of them stay for three months of therapy. A physician also makes regular visits to ensure that their medical needs are being taken care of. Two disability workers have received specialised training in spinal cord injuries from the Association for Physically Disabled in Bangalore. They ensure that the clients are kept busy with a quality exercise program as well as recreational pursuits and wheel-chair mobility skills. Many of the clients are fitted with braces and supplied with crutches or a walker so they can manage at least indoor mobility independently.

I am totally impressed on my visits to see so many of these clients walking with crutches or a walker around the campus grounds. This takes excellent balance skills as well as courage to enable these young men to navigate the grounds and is really a testament to the skills of the rehabilitation workers as well as to the determination of the clients.

Spinal Cord Injured Clients

Two more buildings have been renovated to accommodate these clients with more bathrooms and further ramping and kitchen space. The therapy room is filled with physical activity daily followed by recreational pursuits outside such as ball games and mobility skills. They also have chores to complete such as doing their own laundry and cooking.

Up to this point we are only accepting clients who are paraplegic, not quadriplegic, as there isn't a physiotherapist on staff and the risks are too great for serious medical complications with the higher level injuries. Clients with the higher level injuries are taken care of at home, usually by a family member with weekly visits from one of the disability workers for progression of their exercise program and help with transfers and mobility equipment.

The horticulture program has moved to the spinal cord centre so these clients are now helping with the watering and care of the plants. Further vocational training still needs to be expanded. They have started some computer training as well as tailoring and some simple agricultural tasks such as sewing bags and sorting and bagging seeds. Some of the younger and well-educated clients return to university to continue their studies, once they have learnt how to manage their injuries. As long as the college is accessible, there is no reason why a person with paralysis should not be able to complete their studies and go on to enjoy a career in their chosen field. Unfortunately accessibility issues remain a barrier for many clients.

Some German students spend a year with Samuha each year between graduating from High School and going on to University. This is organised through Civil Service International, Germany. The students work in the Functional Adaptation Program. Their role is to make structural alterations to the home to enable accessibility when a person with disability returns home. This may be building a ramp into the house, or building a toilet room, or just supplying hand-rails, according to the needs.

The medical students from the training college in Koppal have recently taken to visiting this centre so they understand the needs of spinal cord injured clients and can help these clients after the students graduate as doctors.

Samuha Samarthya has received several awards over the years in recognition of their work with the poor in Northern Karnataka. They received two awards in 2017 recognising all the disability rehabilitation services they render in the region. Some of these awards include monetary compensation, which is a great asset to the program.

24

WHERE ARE THEY NOW?

"In a gentle way, you can shake the world."

Mahatma Gandhi

In 2016 Lesley and I returned to Samuha, this time without students. The staff arranged for us to see many of the children who I first met in 1994 when they were struggling with polio. Now they were in their mid-twenties, usefully employed and raising their families. Several of them had chosen to help other people with disability in their work. It was wonderful to see this great progress.

Life is so tough in these villages. Most families struggle to survive in these harsh conditions but when you have an accident and become disabled, it puts a huge strain on the family. Babumiya was lucky to have the support of Samuha. Without this support and without the knowledge of the importance of initial immobilization, he could have been permanently paralysed. The family would then have been left destitute and would have had to rely on the extended family for whatever help they could provide.

Babumiya invited us for dinner at his home. Many members of his family were there and they welcomed us with open arms. He has made great progress in his recovery from the spinal cord injury, when he was tossed by a bullock in 1995. He kept gaining strength over two years then stabilised. Now he has nearly full strength in his right hand but his left hand still has some residual weakness. Some weakness remains in his trunk and in his legs, particularly his right foot but he walks independently with a slight limp. He showed us how busy his paediatric clinic is and invited us to make some new suggestions for therapy. He successfully runs the Samuha Samarthya program in Deodurg and continues to provide therapy both in the early intervention centre and in home visits for clients with spinal cord injury and other disorders. He rides his three-wheeler motorbike to the villages and is totally independent. He has three children, one of whom is a nurse and the other two are mechanics. He is not able to do agriculture work anymore so other members of the family do most of the manual labour to plant and harvest their food.

Babumiya

Virupakshi Hadpad

Virupakshi Hadpad, who I met in 1994 on my first visit to Samuha, when he developed paralysis from polio at two years old and received therapy services as a child, is now 26 years old. He is part of the disability team and he was delighted to tell us that he had received his CBR certification. He makes home and school visits to help children with speech and hearing deficits. He used to travel by bus and walk long distances with his crutch and shoe-raise for his shortened leg.

He joined us when we climbed up the fort above Koppal, which is a steep rocky climb. I was amazed that he could climb this right to the top using one crutch. This was a huge achievement for Virupakshi and is a testament to his determination. He has now moved back to his home in Deodurg and runs the speech and hearing program there. He has his own three-wheeler motor-bike so no longer has to rely on the bus. The Government supplies these motor-bikes to selected candidates, which is a great asset to their lives.

We stopped by and visited Siddappa and found him sitting on the edge of the road outside his tyre repair shop, where he repairs punctures for all kinds of vehicles from bicycles to tractors. He took me for a ride on his three-wheel motor-bike, which has given him a new lease on life. We laughed about how it used to be Samuha giving him a ride and now he was able to take me for a spin! He was one of the first children with polio seen by

Siddappa with author

Samuha, back in 1992. After completing his high school education, he joined Samuha as an orthotic assistant and helped to make braces, similar to those he wore himself to support his legs, enabling him and others to walk with crutches instead of crawling on the ground. He also learnt bicycle repairs. He is totally independent and travels from his home in the village to his shop daily and drives to town to get supplies as needed.

We even went back to Jalahalli to visit Prabhu, who had spinal TB as a child, over twenty years ago, and fully recovered. I was amazed at the huge contrast in his land. Whereas, when I first met him, he lived in a small hut in arid surroundings outside his village. He now has a nice house on irrigated land and has livestock as well as crops. They now have irrigation so the land is fertile and corn and rice were growing on his land. He is married with two young children. The village has grown and a new road has been built to his village so now a jeep can drive right up to his home. Prabhu owns his land and grows enough food to support his family and has cash crops to sell such as rice and corn, so his future is secure.

Dakoji came to the Deodurg clinic to meet us. He drove up on his two-wheeler motor-bike. I first met him when he had polio as a child. At that time he crawled by pulling each foot forwards with his hand. Samuha enabled surgery for him and now he walks independently with one brace. He proudly told me how he is working as a village rehabilitation worker and is responsible for sixty children in thirty eight villages. He also has seven sheep he is rearing to supplement his income. Two years ago he married and has a son. It is wonderful to see how this work has gone full circle with many of our clients, who now help other children with disability.

When we went to Kanakagiri, we visited Durugappa. He was the young boy with Guillaine Barre syndrome who we saw when he was eight years old. At that time, he was too weak to roll over in bed. I met Durugappa again five years later in the market. I could barely recognise him as he had grown and was strong and had a full mop of dark hair. He had completely recovered from Guillaine Barre and was completing his studies. Now he presented as a strong adult who does manual labour in his village.

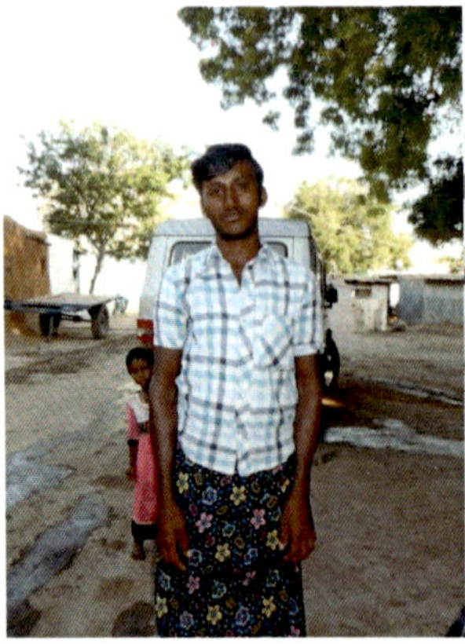
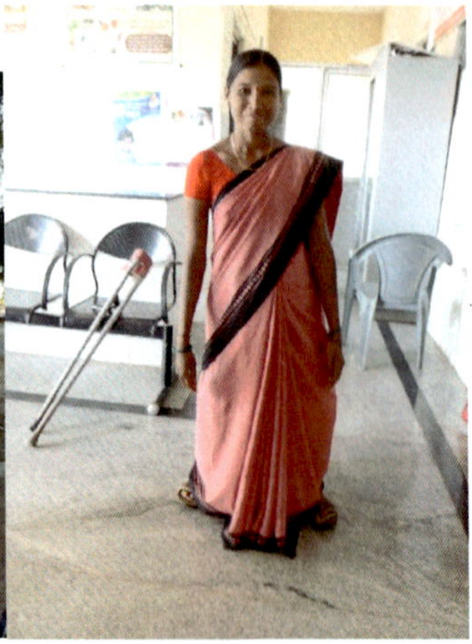

Durugappa *Balavva 1918*

I was so excited to see Balavva. She was the young girl with polio who we first met when she was six years old and her brothers pulled her to school on a small cart. I had seen her a few times since, when she competed in races with her crutches. We travelled to her village, where she is a pre-school teacher and found her at work in the community centre. She was wearing her elegant pink uniform sari and proudly showed me how she could walk down the hallway without any crutches. She beamed triumphantly and informed me that she could walk half a kilometer without her crutches. She also mentioned that she was looking forward to marriage.

We also visited Lakshman, who was a young boy with polio back in 1994 when I first met him. We found him in his shop where he is now a successful tailor and earns a good livelihood through making quality shirts and pants in the village. He also employed an assistant.

I wasn't able to find Ayyamma this time. She was the ten year old girl with severe club foot who travelled independently from her distant village of Tinthini Bridge in order to receive therapy for her foot deformity. However I was told that she now walks with minimal limp without her splint and is happily married with two children.

I hadn't seen Bharathi since she came on our field trips as a young child with polio. It was exciting to see her again after twenty years and to see her being so successful with her life. We found her surrounded by animated children where she is now a pre-school teacher in her village and has twenty six children under her care. She also facilitates government pensions and medicines for families in her village so she is carrying on the good work she learnt through Samuha. She told us she is married with two young children. It was good to see that she no longer needs crutches but uses her caliper.

Another wonderful visit was to see Kaveri, who was the young girl with spina bifida and amputation of the lower left leg. She was now twelve years old and had just received a new prosthesis made by Samarthya. She smilingly showed us how she could walk independently with her artificial limb and didn't need any crutches. She was happy and doing well in school.

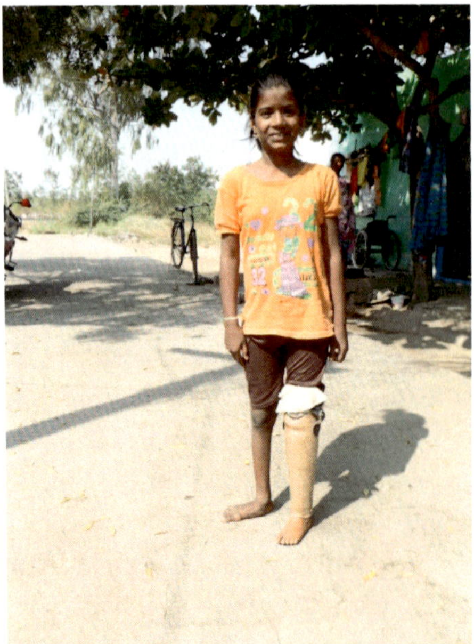

Kaveri

Ashok continues to develop his orthotic skills, having attended several courses. He oversees three orthotic workshops. These workshops are integral to the disability program and Samuha Samarthya continues to work in villages within a sixty kilometre radius of each of these satellite workshops. Clients also come from much farther afield to the centre to receive needed services. Ashok continues to make many artificial limbs for people with amputations. In fact he made forty in 2016 alone.

Ayyalappa is a long-standing member of the Samuha team. He comes from a carpentry background then joined Samuha as a teacher and later joined the disability team. I have a carved elephant on my mantle as a memento from him as well as a wooden chain made from one solid piece of wood. He has worked for Samarthya in many capacities and is a valued member of the team. He is in charge of the functional adaptation program, making homes accessible for clients.

25
REFLECTIONS:

"The future depends on what you do today"

Mahatma Gandhi

Narayanswamy is now the Director of the whole of Samuha so his responsibilities have increased substantially. He married Chitra in 2000 and they have a daughter Kaustubha, who is now a teenager. He brought in Hampanna to Samuha, who is the assistant director of the disability program. Narayanswamy and Hampanna were at college together where they worked with visually impaired clients. Together they have helped Samuha Samarthya grow into the well-respected program it is today.

Narayanswamy and Family

Hampanna has presented at two World Congresses of Physiotherapy on the work of Samuha's Community Based Rehabilitation program, one time in Vancouver and once in Amsterdam. This was the first time he had ever been outside of India and one of the few times he left his state of Karnataka. He found the overseas food difficult and couldn't believe the cost of clothes, when the airline lost his luggage! Hampanna's wife, Sarojamma, runs a tailoring vocational program for people living in poverty and with disability. She runs this out of their house in Koppal. They had two daughters Sweta and Shobha but unfortunately Sweta passed away from Dengue Fever shortly after graduating from teachers college. This was a huge loss to her family, who still struggle with this tragedy. Shobha is doing well in college in Bangalore, studying psychology.

Hampanna and family on top of Koppal Fort

Pradeep is Secretary of Samuha and is still heavily involved in the activities of Samuha. He now lives in Bangalore and runs some entrepreneurial businesses from there. He is working towards developing carbon neutral villages in South India through the implementation of fuel-efficient stoves. However, he is disappointed that the world is slow to embrace the carbon credit program, which could fund some of these initiatives.

The locations of where Samuha works have expanded. Back in 1994, when I first arrived on the scene, the main location was Jalahalli, where there was a large campus from which the CBR program ran. Deodurg, the nearby town, also had a small campus with some rural programs. An orthotic workshop was added in Raichur, the largest city in the District. This workshop still serves this population. The campus in Jalahalli moved outside the village, when the Landlord needed the property. The program ran from there for several years but both of these campuses now have returned to agriculture. A small program still runs out of Deodurg, including one of the CBR programs with orthotic workshop, which is run by Babumiya.

Samuha has since expanded into Koppal, which is now the main centre. This is where the Early Intervention Centre and orthotic workshop are situated and where the Canadian contingent stays when they visit. The spinal cord injury unit is at Irkalgada, situated several kilometers from Koppal and other programs run out of Kanakagiri, several more kilometers distant. All of these locations are situated in Northern Karnataka in South

India. Samuha also initiated an HIV program in Bangalore, called Samraksha, which has now become an independent organisation.

Not only have the clients and Samuha progressed well over this twenty four year period but India has also made great strides in its development. The eradication of polio, was a major accomplishment. It was eradicated in India in 2011 but in Samuha villages since 2004. The pulse polio program will continue until polio is also eradicated in the neighbouring countries. The literacy rate has also improved substantially. The literacy rate in 1994 was only eleven percent in these villages; it is now up to seventy four percent.

In 1994 there were hardly any private vehicles, just the occasional Ambassador sedan. Now there are many cars of all types. The roads have also improved. There is now room to meet and pass a bus without one of the vehicles having to drop down on to the soft shoulder. Back then all the ploughing was done by bullock and simple wooden plough, now it is just as likely to be mechanised as tractors are becoming more common commodities. Even combine harvesters are no longer an uncommon sight.

In the mid-1990s most people grew mixed crops of vegetables for their own use and to sell at the market. More recently land has been bought by rich farmers from neighbouring States, who employ the local farmers to tend their land. Now you see fields of fluffy cotton being grown as well as stretches of bright yellow sunflowers, used for their oil, interspersed with sugarcane and lots of rice. These are cash crops so these can increase the income for the farmer but if the market drops then it is difficult for local farmers to buy food. Previously they were able to store their grains and vegetables for future use. One good thing is that a large canal has been built to provide irrigation for the farmers. This is dry land and they expect drought every third year from lack of rains. This irrigation helps considerably to relieve this problem so families are less vulnerable. The water table however drops to alarming levels in dry years and in 2016 many wells ran dry.

Introduction of large companies into the area has been a problem as traditionally farmers would save seed for their next years' crops but now, with genetic modification, many of their crops don't produce seed so this puts them at great hardship for having to rely on outside companies. There is also the danger of lack of biodiversity, increasing the vulnerability of the farmer.

When I first visited India I never saw Kentucky Fried Chicken or McDonalds. There was no Coca Cola, instead India had their own brand called Thumbs-Up. Everything was wrapped in newspaper and the merchants made their own bags out of newspaper. Now, with globalisation, all of these western companies are prevalent and plastic bags are more commonly used.

On one occasion, when visiting Deodurg, Babumiya planned a plastic bag clean-up drive in the town. Several of us walked down the streets with garbage bags and picked up all the plastic garbage in the neighbourhood. We then deposited all the bags in front of the Municipal Offices while carrying signs decrying the use of plastic bags and chanting "No more plastic," in Kanadda. It felt good to participate in an environmental rally in India.

The amount of traffic on the roads has increased substantially, especially in the cities but animals are still herded down the streets and bicycles and motor-bikes and auto-rickshaws are still common. Bangalore now has a mono-rail commuter system but the streets are still crowded with people and vehicles.

The trains haven't changed at all. They are still the most efficient way of moving from A to B. The sleeping berths are still hard and narrow. Most people travel this way on overnight trains to reach their appointments and carry on their business. Amazingly they appear refreshed.

I learnt to use a computer in Jalahalli in 1994 although there was no phone and often no electricity. Now nearly everyone has a smart phone. It's not uncommon to be driving through a village and seeing the local farmers, dressed in their home-spun traditional dhoti, chatting on their phones. It is wonderful to see the speech and hearing impaired people carrying on animated conversations using sign language through their video calls. For a minimal monthly fee, all calls within India are free and 1 GB of data is provided free daily. This is an amazing contrast compared to the two hour jeep drive needed to access an international phone service back in 1994.

Most of the villages still don't have indoor plumbing and still collect their water from a communal bore-well.
Recently I read a notice in the newspaper saying,
"Open defecation is banned in Koppal District but is still acceptable in Raichur District as there aren't enough public toilets there yet."
A few days later a notice read,
"Anyone seen defecating in Koppal District will be publicly shamed and named."

Electricity is much more prevalent now but in many areas there is no power for six hours during the day, as the system cannot produce enough for everyone. Most of the electricity is still produced from coal.

In Koppal, we have a western toilet for western visitors and for people with disability. They have a bidet type hand held sprayer for personal hygiene as they don't use paper. In order to have a hot shower, you place a heating element in a bucket of water for ten minutes and voila – you have a bucket of hot water, which is plenty for a jug and bucket bath, even enough to wash your hair. You just have to make sure you don't test the temperature while the coil is still in the water!

The disability program has expanded from our original team of five CBR workers to the present team of twenty-seven. We have moved beyond polio to seeing everyone of any age with any kind of disability. There is a large Speech and Hearing Program for helping children with hearing loss to manage in school and for provision of hearing aids. The Braille teacher helps the visually impaired and the team are also trained in mobility training, including the use of a white cane. SODA is mostly involved with helping those with physical disabilities, in particular the early intervention program for children under six and the social rehabilitation centre for adults with spinal cord injury, but we also help clients with all kinds of disabilities.

It took SODA a few years to reach our goal of sending $10,000.00 annually to Samuha to help them run their program. We then expanded our goal to $20,000.00 annually, which we still attain but frequently we have been sending over $30,000.00 each year. Most of our funds are raised through our annual dinner and auction. We also give some talks to high schools and other groups, as requested. We sell Indian recipe books and we developed a brochure where donors can identify how they would like their funds to be used, eg: for a wheel-chair or braces or a course of treatment.

S.O.D.A. Executive

Recently Samuha has started using the term "Difability", derived from differently abled. The following quote from Hampanna in his foreword for The Stars Amidst The Golden Rays by Dr JS Aswath Kumar states,
"----this position is rooted in our belief that difability as a development issue is not primarily the result of physical or mental differences but is the result of society hindering and disabling (not enabling) people and children who deviate from the social norm."

This philosophy illustrates Samuha's progressive way of thinking and is at the core of how they run their program.

In Germany, youth have the choice of two years national service or two years of social service, which can be taken overseas. I believe that all people from industrial nations should spend time volunteering in a developing country, not just to help out, but also to experience how the majority of people live and understand the great disparity in wealth throughout the world. Through greater understanding we should be better prepared to help solve global problems. This should be a two way sharing of ideas and information.

I am so thankful that I conquered my fears and accepted the contract to work with Samuha back in 1994. So many opportunities have presented themselves due to this overseas experience in India, such as teaching in Bhutan and joining a medical team in both Tibet and Ladakh. These have all been life-changing and enriching experiences. My involvement with Samuha in India has deepened my knowledge and broadened my life considerably. It is good to seize a moment of adversity as an opportunity. Stepping out of one's comfort zone can bring unexpected rewards.

Floyd and I continue to lead active lives. We have renovated our log home ourselves and enjoy curling, dancing, gardening and canoeing together and of course our ever-expanding family gatherings. We are still free to follow our own pursuits such as my annual trips to India, writing retreats and hiking while Floyd continues to enjoy his endeavours. He has become one of the most generous supporters of S.O.D.A. and takes every opportunity to show his pride and respect for our work.

We can learn much from others in the majority world. How hoarding of wealth and possessions has nothing to do with happiness or life fulfillment. As Akong Rinpoche said in Tibet, “Westerners are drowning in consumption.” He is so right. However, we are fortunate to have a social security net to help us in times of need.

Another good philosophy to remember from David Werner, when designing programs for people with disability is, “Nothing about us without us”
but Mahatma Gandhi should have the last word,
“Be the change you want to see in the world.” and “Live simply so that others may simply live.”

Gandhi

The complexities of India:
The most noble leader of our time is spawned
He led his countrymen from British rule
to Independence dawn

He led by example, a simplistic life
Non-violence was his creed
another sin he abhorred was greed

A spinning wheel and an acre of land,
He espoused the needs of every man
Instead of this the rich have more
While others struggle – forever poor.

Republic Day – SAMUHA - Koppal 1918

SODA's website: www.samuha.ca
Samuha's disability program website:
www.samarthya.org
Both of these websites have photos, videos and stories of Samuha's work.

All profits from the sale of this book go to support Samuha's Disability Program.

GLOSSARY:

- **SAMUHA** - Integrated development organisation in India.
- **SAMARTHYA** – Disability Program of SAMUHA
- **S.O.D.A.** – Samuha Overseas Development Association – charity based in Prince George, Canada, which supports Samarthya's work.

- **CBR** - Community Based Rehabilitation
- **EIC** - Early Intervention Centre
- **SCI** - Spinal Cord Injury

TABLE OF RE-APPEARING CHARACTERS:

Author's family:

- **Floyd** – husband
- **Helen** – sister
- **Brenda** - daughter

SAMUHA **Samarthya staff and clients:**

- **Narayanswamy, NS** – wife Chitra, daughter Kostubha. Initially Director of Disability program. Now Director of Samuha
- **Pradeep** – Founder of Samuha
- **Hampanna** - Assistant Director of Samarthya, Disability Programme

Ashok – Senior orthotic technician

Kallappa – 1st Disability worker

Chandamma – Disability worker, suicide
Babumiya – Disability worker, developed spinal cord injury
Ayyalappa – Disability worker
Juliette - Occupational Therapy volunteer
Siddappa – client with polio
Ayyamma – child with club foot
Prabhu – child with TB spine
Mounesh – child with TB spine
Virupakshi – child with polio, and disability worker
Dakoji – child with polio
Bavvamma – client with polio
Durugappa – child with Guillaine Barre Syndrome
Kaveri - child with spina bifida and amputation

SODA members and students:
Lesley – several visits, physiotherapist
Colleen – one visit, born in Calcutta, RN
Elaine – one visit, RN
Andrea – 3 visits, student physiotherapist, preceptor.

Vocabulary:
Caliper - Leg brace
Namaskara - Greeting with folded hands
Oota - Food
Nasta - Breakfast
Chai wallah - Tea seller
Guru - Spiritual Teacher